ONE
HEAD
MANY
HATS

ONE
HEAD
MANY
HATS

ROBERT D BREWER

BROWN
DOG
BOOKS

First published 2018

Copyright © Robert D. Brewer 2018

The right of Robert D. Brewer to be identified as the author of this work has been asserted in accordance with the Copyright, Designs & Patents Act 1988.

Published under licence by Brown Dog Books and
The Self-Publishing Partnership, 7 Green Park Station, Bath BA1 1JB

www.selfpublishingpartnership.co.uk

ISBN printed book: 978-1-78545-342-7

ISBN e-book: 978-1-78545-343-4

Cover design by Kevin Rylands
Internal design by Andrew Easton

Printed and bound by CPI Group (UK) Ltd, Croydon, CR0 4YY

One Head Many Hats

Thank you to my wonderful wife Sue, for assisting me in this book. Your suggestions have been invaluable, and one day I hope I'm able to repeat the process for you.

Thanks to my two daughters, Gemma and Sophie for their advice, especially regarding the book covers. Lol.

And lastly, in memory to my dear departed mum. If there is a heaven, then I'm sure she's up there looking down and telling everyone in a proud voice, "that's my Robert."

CHAPTER 1

My earliest memory was at the day nursery at Stanhope School in Greenford, Middlesex, and I must have been about three years old. I remember swallowing a marble while lying in a cot, and then turning onto my side and coughing the marble out. Not a particularly big marble, but big enough to choke on. Natural instincts kicked in, even at such an early age: knowing how to cough when something is lodged in the back of your throat. Early memories of the nursery were of the ladies who looked after us. I've since seen pictures, old black and white ones, of these ladies in their pinnies cuddling us toddlers.

I lived in a two-bedroom ground-floor maisonette with my mum, Eleanor Brewer, and my granddad, George Brewer, in Greenford. My mum had had a hard life, having lost her mum, Florence Brewer, when she was six years old. Mum would often comment on her loss, saying she could never remember her mum. She was bought up by my granddad who was a veteran of the First World War. He had served in the Royal Horse Artillery, riding the horses that pulled the artillery guns up to the front line. He had had a hard life as well, having lost his wife at an early age, and then having to bring up a six-year-old girl, my mum, on his own. This was in the 1940s and my mum went through her life without having the caring bond that a mother can bring to her child.

I was an illegitimate brown boy, my father having been a black

American serviceman who met my mum in London in 1954, and they produced me in 1955. After I was born he was posted back to the U.S. of A., so I never ever got to meet him. I never really got a straight answer from my mum when I asked her about my dad. So over the years I just accepted the fact that I had no father and got on with my life. My father's name was Robert Brown and he was a private first-class in the US Army. Mum had his US Army number, rank and name on a piece of paper, having kept it for sentimental reasons.

As an adult some years later, and with the assistance of the US Military Department, I managed to trace a man with my father's name and service number and still living in the town that we believed my father came from, which was Wilmington in Delaware. During this time I wrote a letter to him, but I didn't receive a reply. I wasn't too disappointed (well, maybe just a little).

I went to Ravenor Park Infants School, which was just around the corner from where we lived. At the age of four my first teacher was Mrs Smith, and I remember sitting on the floor in her classroom with all the other children. I got bored and distracted easily at an early age and therefore got up to mischief at every opportunity. My second teacher was Miss Parker and she made me sit in the front of the class opposite her desk so she could keep an eye on me. I must have been five going on six years old at the time.

She always called me 'Robert Brewer' in a stern manner and rarely called me just 'Robert'.

On her 'star chart', which highlighted the achievements of the schoolchildren, I probably had the least amount of gold stars awarded for good work in the class. During playtime I was always made to stand by the naughty wall, which in those days was an old air-raid shelter stuck in the middle of the playground. I never knew why I had to stand by the naughty wall, but it was probably for misbehaving in some way.

Looking back, my problem was that no one actually sat me down and explained anything to me. I was just punished for misbehaving and had to pay the consequences. I don't think I ever managed a whole playtime in that year without enduring the naughty wall.

By the time I was seven years old I was probably stigmatised as a 'problem half-caste boy'. I continued to underachieve at primary school, learning very little compared to the rest of my classmates.

I started a milk round at about ten years old. I was the milk boy for two different milkmen, both of whom had the first name of Ted. One was called Little Ted and the other Big Ted, because one was short and the other big, hence their nicknames.

They worked for Express Dairies, and their milk depot was situated in Greenford, about a mile from where I lived. Later on, they reallocated the depot to Northolt which was about three miles away from Greenford. I delivered milk to families in my road and to the surrounding streets, and I alternated between the two milkmen, working for Little Ted for three weekends in a row, then one weekend for Big Ted.

At the beginning I just worked weekends, starting at 7 in the morning and finishing at around 3 in the afternoon on a Saturday and about 11am on the Sunday. Saturday was collection day for the weekly milk money from the customers, which meant I made a load of money through tips. I was probably around 11 or 12 years old when I started to drive the electric milk float. It was easier for both Teds, and we both took turns in driving the float on the milk round.

In those days, nearly every house in the street had milk delivered from their local milkman. So in essence I would deliver to a few houses on one side of the street, and Ted would deliver on the other side. So whoever finished first would walk back to the float and drive 30 or so yards and start again with the delivery of milk and produce like butter, cream and eggs to the next row of houses.

I had my own milkman's hat, apron and money satchel. My wages would be 10 shillings (that's 50p in today's money) from Little Ted, and 15 shillings (75p) from Big Ted. Although there was a major difference in pay, I enjoyed working for both milkmen equally. Of course I had the tips from the customers which boosted my wages considerably. By this time I got to know all the customers who tipped, and would ensure that I delivered to these customers on payday. Both Teds also knew who tipped and encouraged the arrangement whereby I would receive the tips.

During the mid to late 60s, every boy had a part-time job. It was either a milk round, a paper round, a Corona round delivering fizzy drinks, or the baker's round. There were even boys delivering paraffin off the back of a flatbed lorry to people's houses. The paraffin was stored in a big steel drum which had a tap connected to it, and the paraffin was served to customers via a large, metal jug. Health & Safety would have had a field day, but we were happy and I never heard of anyone ever getting injured.

Around this time I was the school goalkeeper and my football suffered badly because I could only play midweek games. I had an outstanding game one afternoon against the best school team in the area. I was about 11 years old and we were expected to get hammered, but we only lost 1-0 due to me playing the game of my life. There was a football scout watching the game and he invited me to play for the Ealing Borough Football Team the following Saturday. The Borough team were playing a better side who had beaten us 3-1 in a previous game. I didn't have a great game, but we drew 1-1 which was a better result than the last time the two teams had met. After the game, the coach asked me if I could play again for the Borough the following week.

I said that I couldn't because I had to do my milk round that weekend. As I had already let Ted down once I couldn't risk letting him down again the following week. Christ, I was only 11: what did I know?

My first big regret in life was that I didn't pursue the football. I was good but I didn't take it too seriously and probably missed out. I also had no one to push or advise me, as my male role models at the time were Little Ted and Big Ted, and of course they wanted me to pursue a career as a milkman.

I was a Life Boy when I was eight. They were the junior members of the Boys' Brigade and we would meet at the local Baptist church at the top of my road. I'm not sure why, I think it was because most of my school friends were Boy Cubs that I had joined the Cubs shortly afterwards. They were situated at the local Methodist church about a mile away. I then became a Boy Scout and ended up as a patrol leader with the Buffalos Patrol. I liked the Scouts, as I could rough-and-tumble to my heart's content.

CHAPTER 2

I left the Junior School, and without surprising anyone I failed the 11-plus exam, which confirmed whether you went to the grammar school or the secondary modern school. I went to Stanhope Secondary Modern for Boys and then spent the next four years bored out of my mind. The highlights of my distinguished school career were that the Maths teacher painstakingly showing me how Maths worked. I am eternally grateful to that gentleman: he never caned any of the schoolboys but ruled by respect. A rare commodity nowadays.

Unfortunately this cannot be said for the Geography teacher. He had no such reservations regarding 'sparing the rod'. He used his cane on me with great pleasure for talking in class on one occasion. He gave me two strokes on each hand, well on my upper wrist, actually. I was 12 years old at the time and Mum hit the roof when she saw the cane marks on my wrists. She went to the school the next day to confront the teacher. He would have been arrested for ABH, Assault Occasioning Actual Bodily Harm, today, but I never talked in his class again. Lesson learnt?

It's really hard to grasp the fact that corporal punishment, as it was called, was totally acceptable in the 1960s. In those days the main form of punishment was caning, using a bamboo cane on the backside or on the open palms of the hands. The secondary choice of punishment tool was the good old slipper applied to the schoolboy's bottom. This was often the favourite punishment tool amongst the PE teachers. Amazingly, this was legal.

I played badminton at school in my first year and was one of the better players in my class. In my first knock-out competition, I reached the final and was due to play against another boy who was also in my class. Everyone thought he would beat me, as he had all the kit and an expensive racket, but I knew I could beat him, and I did.

I went on to represent the school in many badminton competitions and won a few trophies during my time as a seasoned player. I realised from an early age that just because someone looks the part it doesn't necessarily mean they are the real thing.

In my second year at school I was put into the dunces' class, because I wasn't working hard enough and was spending most of the time misbehaving or just daydreaming. I worked like hell that year to get out of that class, but it took two years to eventually escape and be upgraded to the intermediate class.

I recall attending Physics classes for four years, and during those years I played chess at the back of the class with all the other no-hopers. So my chess improved immeasurably, but my Physics tuition went slowly downhill. I never really excelled at anything other than sport and as I was labelled a 'problem boy', I lived up to my notoriety by continually messing about.

After being caned on the hand several times and getting the slipper on the backside on a regular basis, I became immune to pain. So at the ripe old age of 13, there was no deterrent for my bad behaviour. My poor mum used to dread school parent evenings. "He must do better, he can do better, Robert must try harder," was perpetually repeated by all the teachers to my mother's shame and embarrassment.

I was in the 3rd year, so must have been 13 or 14 years old, and a form teacher who had little control over us gave me detention for something which I hadn't done, which was humming in class. He tried to get me to admit to the humming and said he would cancel the detention if I admitted to the offence. I was so stubborn I wouldn't admit to doing something that I hadn't done, so I did the detention.

The irony was that I had hummed in the class on previous occasions, just not on that particular time. Maybe it was restorative justice kicking in. I'm not sure what lesson I learnt because detention was a total waste of time. Writing out 100 lines, "I must not etc etc", was not going to deter anyone.

Years later, I was sorting through my departed mum's papers and came across my old school reports. They were not pleasant reading. It was a similar theme throughout, mainly negative and mainly on my part. I often reflect on my wasted school years as I failed school and they failed me – or was it the case of leave the problem ones behind and concentrate on the promising ones. To this day I'm not quite sure what the right course is for the schools to take.

It took me many years to realise that in life if you had a reputation you would continually live up to your notoriety. The powers that be would allow and even encourage that 'name tag', so they could justify themselves in labelling you a 'problem child' in the first place.

Each year my home town would hold an annual fete, and I went to the fete one year when I was an adult, and after I had achieved many things in my life. My mum was a volunteer victim support worker at the time and they had a stall at the fete trying to raise money for their organisation. Whilst there, as you do, I had a wander around the numerous stalls on display. There was usual mixture of 'Lucky This', 'Throw n Win a Fish/Toy' etc. I was drawn to one stall that had the name of my old secondary school on it. I instantly recognised the teacher who was in charge of the stall, it was one of my old PE teachers. I started to talk to him and unsurprisingly he remembered me, as they always remembered the naughty ones. He was amazed when I told him what my current profession was and what I had done in the past. He was the headmaster then and I felt rather smug with myself, because I'm sure he had me down as a candidate for HMP Wormwood Scrubs.

I was about 14 and I lived for football and badminton. Both little Ted and big Ted had left and I found myself working for a number of other milkmen on a variety of milk rounds. Although they were all kind to me, I was realising that working all day Saturday was preventing me from playing footie and having fun with my mates.

I ended up getting a morning paper round and also an evening paper round. I delivered the daily papers to streets near me every morning and the *Evening News* and the *Evening Standard* to homes in the local area. I also had an evening wine round for a short while. Although it was named "wine", it was more beer and spirits.

I'd deliver locally on a bicycle which was a big, black monster of a thing. It had a small front wheel and a big back wheel. The bike had one speed, no brakes, and a great big, wooden crate fixed to the front where the drinks would be stored, and it was a death trap.

Unsurprisingly, I received a disproportionate number of tips because the majority of the recipients liked their drink and were always rather merry when I arrived with their purchases.

I started smoking at around this time, nicking the odd fag from my mum's pack. The first time I inhaled a cigarette I was sitting on a small garden wall at the top of our street. After the first initial inhaling, I started to feel all wheezy and nearly fainted and fell off the wall. After that I was hooked on the fags for the next nine years, give or take.

As most young lads do, I joined a gang. We weren't really that infamous, just getting into the odd fight, and generally misbehaving and getting into trouble. A few of the boys got involved in drugs and one ended up as a burglar. I know this for a fact because one afternoon I caught him in our house trying to steal my mum's Green Shield Stamps books. I had come home early and caught him in the kitchen with the books in his hands. I wasn't too pleased.

Before the discovery of glue sniffing, we discovered an equally dangerous form of achieving a 'high'. I won't mention what the product was as it's easily obtained and if used incorrectly like we did, then the repercussions could be quite serious. We would take this @@@@ and receive what we famously called the 'buzz'. This buzz took the feeling of invincibility and of great wonderment. It would last for a few minutes after which you'd start the process again. The problem was that we often got involved in fights and because of the buzz you didn't feel any pain.

The next morning was a different matter because you felt like s@@t.

The other problem was that the more you took, the longer it took to get the buzz. Luckily I realised the stupidity and stopped taking it. Unfortunately not all were as lucky as I was, as I heard years later that at least one of the gang had died early due to a drugs overdose.

I recall the first time I was called Spade. I was around 13, and one afternoon after finishing school, I'd walked over to my local park for a game of football. It was the type of place where you could always get a game. There were several football pitches and there were games going on between the pitches.

As I was walking along, I heard a voice shout out, 'Spade, ow Spade!' You know what it's like when you hear someone shouting, you always turn around through curiosity. So I looked over and saw this boy, whom I vaguely knew, gesticulating towards me. I wandered over and was asked if I fancied making up the numbers. The boy's name nickname was Stosh and he was two years older than me, but about my size. As to the rest of the motley group of players, they were made up of the usual ragamuffins who wanted a game of footie but were not good enough to get picked for a decent match.

So the sides were quickly picked, about seven in each team, and with coats and bags as goalposts and an imaginary pitch. Every boy growing up knew when the ball was out even when there were no markings: we just made it up. The main thing was not to be the last player to be picked for a team, as it was so humiliating. Surprisingly, Stosh picked me about fourth, saying, "Spade, you're on my side." So off we went with the kick-off. I played OK against predominantly older kids. Someone always shouts, "Half-time!" – there were no refs or linesmen (sorry, referee's assistants) in those days.

The second half kicked off, and the score was about equal between the two teams. Then someone always shouts, "Next goal's the winner!" I remember getting the ball, beating about three opposition players and all I had was Fatty, the goalie, to beat. He was wearing a yellow Gordon Banks goalie shirt, baggy shorts and odd socks, one up and one down. I cracked the ball in the top left-hand corner: Goal!! Don't forget there were no nets in those days, we judged if it was a goal or not and that was definitely a goal!!

"Spade, that was great!" "Brilliant, Spade!" were just two of the plaudits that were bestowed on me by Stosh and the rest of the team. As we made our way home, someone shouted out, "See you next week, Spade!" I felt as though I had won the World Cup.

It was a late afternoon a few days later when there was a knock on the door and my mum was saying, "Who's that at the door?" How was I supposed to know? So I got off the sofa and opened the door and saw Stosh standing there with his mum, who was a big, empowering woman. I could also see that Stosh had a big red mark on the side of his face.

Now, every boy growing up in this era had an uncanny psychic ability to transfer a warning to another: it was, 'you're in trouble' or 'we're in trouble'. I thought of a number of misdemeanours that I was guilty of. The aim was to admit to the one least likely to get you into too much trouble. But I was mystified, as I knew that I hadn't been up to wrongdoings with Stosh.

My mum then came to the door wanting to know what all the fuss was about. Then Stosh's mum said, "Go on, go on, apologise." Stosh then said, "Sorry, Robert, for calling you Spade." He looked at me and I looked at him with a 'what the f@@k is this all about?' His mum then said, "I won't have that sort of language in our house, he's got it from his elder brother and I won't have it." She was saying that Stosh kept going on about "Spade this and Spade that". Stosh and I both were dumbfounded. After this, he got another slap from his mum and then they both left.

I had no idea what the problem was until sometime later when I was informed that Spade was not only a garden tool, or a playing card suit, but was also a derogatory term for a person of colour.

Many, many years later after I moved away, I popped into my old local pub after visiting my mum. The year must have been early 2000, and I'd only been in there for a few moments when I heard a voice say, "Hey, Spade." There was a late lunchtime clientele with a few workers having a liquid lunch. The noise level dropped to silence, the barman stopped cleaning his beer glass, the piano player stopped playing… You get the gist.

I looked around and saw a skinny, little fellow, wearing a council workman's donkey jacket, holding up a beer and smiling. 35-plus years on, I'd recognise that scrawny face and smile anywhere. Stosh. He obviously recognised me, and I recognised him, luckily for him. We both burst out laughing and had a chat about the good old times.

I was to learn many a lesson about comments of a racist nature in my life. I personally believe that it's not what you say but who says it, and in what context, and most importantly, what the motive is. When Stosh called me 'Spade' all those years ago, it was never meant to be offensive and I never took it to be anything more than a nickname.

CHAPTER 3

I had no inclination about joining the Army. No one in my family had served in Her Majesty's Forces other than my grandfather, as previously mentioned.

It was the summer holidays of 1971, and I had just scraped enough exam marks to go on to 5th year at school. I was at the local park hanging about with some mates when I was asked by one of them if I'd go to the Army Careers Office in Wembley with him. He said he'd pay for my bus ride and would also buy me a Wimpy if I went with him. He just wanted some moral support.

So off we went to the Army Careers Office and somehow I ended up taking the entrance exam with him. I passed the initial exam and was told by the Army recruitment sergeant that I had scored enough points to join the Queen's Regiment. I had no idea who or what they were, but they sounded impressive. When I went home and told my mum that I was going to join the Army and not go back to school, she had an almighty fit and hit the roof. After all, I was only 15 years old.

It was a battle of wills, because I needed her to sign the papers giving permission for me to join, as I was a minor, being under 18 years of age. Of course she initially refused to sign. I told her that I wasn't going back to school and she said, "Well you had better get a job or you're out." Bless her, she kicked me out and I slept in a mate's shed, which was just up the top of our street for a couple of nights.

Although it was summertime, it was cold at night in that shed. My mate's parents didn't know they had a visitor and he would bring me a cup of tea and a sandwich first thing each morning. Then I slept on a stairwell in a block of flats for a couple more nights, after my mate's parents started to get suspicious. Apparently, they couldn't understand how their food stocks were diminishing so quickly.

As fate would have it, I had spent a fair amount of time in the local library now that I had left school, and found books to be quite enlightening. I saw mum by chance in there late afternoon on day 5 of my misadventure. She didn't see me and I could see that she looked awful with worry. I felt really bad, even though at the time I was a selfish git who only thought of himself.

So that evening I went back home, not quite knowing what reaction I'd get from her. Bless her, she hugged me and started to cry. She then ran me a bath because she said that I stank, and afterwards she made me a big dinner. This was very well received because my diet for the previous five days had been chips and snacks. What us sons put our mother's through.

Afterwards, we both sat down and I explained that I had no desire to go back to school and that I just wanted to join the Army. She relented and signed the papers, giving her permission for me to join up. I went back to the Army Careers Office with her written permission and I waited to hear back from them. In the meantime I had to get a job.

Shortly afterwards, I was at the local park again (that bloody park) with some mates and someone said that 'Pikes', a butcher's wholesalers in Greenford, were looking for general labourers. In those days there was no filling out of application forms online, you just turned up and asked if there were any jobs going. Oh, the simplicity of it all.

The place was situated just off the High Street in Greenford, and I went along and saw the owner and asked if there was any work. My job interview consisted of the owner pointing to the leg of a cow, which was on the back of a truck, and telling me to lift it off and take it into the fridge, which was situated at the back of the warehouse. I was big and strong for my age and so passed the interview with flying colours, and got a job as general labourer.

Our nickname was Yob because we yobbed/lobbed, masses of meat around for the butchers to cut up. There were two other lads who were slightly older than me, and they showed me the ropes.

It was a great job for a young man, lifting and carrying great amounts of meat around for the butchers. I was only there for about five months and had a great time. Starting at 6 every morning and finished at 3 in the afternoon. I was paid about £5 per week, which was a fortune for a 15-year-old in those days.

There was a top butcher there at the time called Joe. He was a big, menacing Jamaican, who stood for no nonsense from us young yobs. He would regularly lock us in the freezer or threaten us with his carving knives if we mucked about. A great character.

Christmas time of 1971 and the staff were told by the owner to help themselves to any meat that we wanted in the walk-in fridge. The only stipulation was that we had to be able to carry what we wanted and not use any bags of trolleys. I got a turkey so big it wouldn't fit in the oven, and a massive piece of pork that lasted us for two weeks together with a couple of pounds of sausages and bacon. Many years later, my Aunty Ann, whom we would visit at Christmas time, always remarked about the size of that turkey, and we all had a great laugh.

I received a letter from the Army to attend Wembley Careers Office to take my Ascertation. This is the ceremony where you swear allegiance to The Queen and after which you receive a small bible (I've still got mine). It was the 6th of December 1971 and I was six days short of my 16th birthday.

I didn't return to Pikes after Christmas of 71 because I got my start date to join the Army. I told Mr Pike and he wished me every success in my new career.

So in the second week of January 1972, I started training as a junior soldier at Bassingbourn Barracks just outside Cambridge. I think Don McLean's 'American Pie' was in the pop charts.

I arrived at Royston railway station in Cambridge, and was taken to the Army barracks in an old green Army coach together with a couple of lads of a similar age. We arrived at the Army camp and were ordered to go to a nearby barrack block. I remember queuing in line with a number of other lads, all my age.

At the front of the queue were two corporals who were seated at a desk. They were delegating which platoon each young lad would be assigned to. This was either 4 Platoon or 5 Platoon. As I got nearer to the desk, it was evident that the corporals were alternating the boys between 4 and 5. There were two lads in front of me who knew each other and wanted to be in the same platoon together.

So they asked if I could queue between them, thus ensuring that whatever platoon they were allocated to, they would be together. So when I got to the desk I was allocated to 4 Platoon. If I had stayed in my original position in the queue then I would have gone to 5 Platoon.

4 Platoon's Sergeant was a giant of a man called Sgt Kay-Lesser, or Sgt KL, as he was fondly known. We knew he would not stand for any shenanigans from the young lads. A typical Army sergeant, he was both intimidating and inspiring at the same time to us youngsters. He also had a sense of humour and was a father figure to us all.

As I'd been a Boy Scout and experienced numerous camping holidays, I was used to sleeping away from home. So I wasn't too perplexed about being away from my mum.

My first barrack room consisted of sharing with nine other boys. I soon realised that the boys from up north – Birmingham, Manchester, Liverpool, Newcastle etc – were harder than us southerners. We were a mixture of the Queen's Regiment (mainly southerners), the Royal Anglians (from the East of England) (nicknamed the Farmers) and the Royal Regiment of Fusiliers (mainly northerners).

The first 12 weeks of Army life was called Basic Training. Learning how to march as a platoon and the basics of being a soldier. Army life for a junior soldier started at 0630 when we were loudly awakened by one of the corporals with the dawn chorus of, "Hands off cocks, on with socks and stop wanking. Come on, you 'orrible lot, up you get!" It wasn't for delicate souls. Other comical phrases that raised a laugh were, "I'm your mother now, make your mum proud" and "Am I hurting you? 'Cause I'm standing on your hair", and a vast array of comical idioms designed to raise a discreet chuckle, unless of course you were directly in the firing line.

I could never get my head around the 'first fag of the day was always best'. I think everyone smoked in those days, but some would light up as soon as their feet were on the cold floor of the barrack room. Personally I couldn't light up before my breakfast. This was always a fry-up and a mug of tea (NATO Standard, which was milk and two sugars).

The Army insisted on a certain way to make your bed in the morning during basic training. It was called a bed block. It consisted of three blankets and the two sheets folded neatly in a two-foot square. Then finally the pièce de résistance would be the fourth blanket carefully folded around the three blankets and the two sheets to make a nice secure bed block.

I know some young soldiers took their bed blocks to new levels. So meticulous was the creation that they would sleep on their beds with no sheets or blankets and lay the bed block to the side of their bed ready for the next day's inspection. The corporals took great delight in destroying your masterpiece on the regular room inspections.

Three good meals a day with plenty of activities was just up my street. After our early evening dinner at around 5pm, there were always compulsory activities for an hour or two afterwards. It consisted of sports such as boxing, football and badminton, and this was held in a giant, old aircraft hangar that had been converted into a gym. We could indulge in plenty of exercises and sports, and burn off any extra energy. After that, there was always supper, which consisted of leftovers from dinner. I got on with everyone in the platoon, but I also realised that I could be fine in my own company. My problem was that I always had to have the last word.

Another activity that the Army subscribed to was outward-bound activities such as climbing and potholing. My first encounter with these two activities highlighted an inner fear that I would develop over many years.

I indulged like most young boys with tree climbing, but it didn't really appeal to me like it did for some of the others. My first adventure as a young soldier in the Army was being taken to Sheffield for a week, and alternating between rock climbing one day and potholing the next.

I didn't particularly like heights but managed to conquer those fears, but potholing, no way. I realised at an early age I didn't like being underground. My first and lasting experience of potholing was going down a hole called 'Giants' in Sheffield. It didn't help because the group I was in was led by an officer who got us lost. It wasn't for long and we eventually saw that marvellous light at the end of the tunnel.

But from the age of 16, tunnels made me tremble. So in later years in the Army, when on exercise, and when I had to dig and sleep in a trench, it took all my resolve to overcome my fears. In later years I accepted my phobia and just shrugged it off. Tunnels were not for me unless I really had to. No way would I go into any form of trench or down a hole unless absolutely necessary.

I was paid £2 per week, and every Thursday there would be pay parade. We would singly march into the platoon officer's room, halt, salute, receive our wages and say, "Pay and paybook correct, sir", salute, and march out. Off to the NAAFI (local Army shop) I would go, where I would buy 100 No. 10 cigarettes, a bottle of pop, a sticky bun or similar, and a small war comic. I would read the comic then sell it on. After my purchases, I would have approximately 20 pence left. This would be my emergency funds for when I ran out of cigarettes, which was usually by the following Tuesday. We managed on our wages because we were frugal and had respect for others and ourselves. If one of us was short of fags, then someone would help out.

I think my mum passed this on to me. Every Friday evening, she would divvy up her wage packet. So much for food, rent, electric, etc, then a little left over for emergencies.

A famous saying in the Army was 'twos up'. Nothing of a sexual nature, it meant sharing. So you'd share a fag, a bottle of pop, a bun etc with your opo (best mate) after he asked for 'twos up'. Come Thursday morning prior to pay parade, it wasn't unusual for a single fag to be passed around by four or five other junior soldiers. The last recipient getting a 'fives up'.

During my time as a junior soldier, we were all given education classes for two mornings a week. We were taught by Army education officers, captains usually, and studied English, Maths and a variety of other subjects. There was no messing about and we wore our best BDs – battledress – for all classes and of course our best boots.

The Army loved shiny boots, and to get them to the required standard we would 'bull' them. We would spend hours 'bulling' our boots, it was quite therapeutic. We called it a 'bulling circle', a bit like a knitting circle, and we would all have a chat and a smoke and compare each other's boots.

I think I learnt more in one year as a junior soldier than all my combined time at secondary school. After my basic training was completed, we had our 'passing-out parade'. It was held on a massive disused airfield at the back of the barracks and it was freezing. It was where all the mums and dads would travel to from all over the country to see their sons 'pass out' from their basic training. My mum made it, not an easy journey for her as she had to rely on the trains and buses to get to the parade. I swear I could hear her telling everyone in a loud and proud voice, "That's my Robert." Despite the fact that all the other mums and dads were there to see their sons pass out.

Two things stayed with me on that day and were to shape my life in more ways than I could have ever have imagined. When 4 Platoon and 5 Platoon were lined up ready to march on parade, the Junior Corps of Drums appeared. I had never seen or heard them before. Looking back, they were the smartest soldiers I had ever seen. They looked immaculate and sounded fantastic as they marched between the aircraft hangars and onto the parade ground.

I had no musical aspirations in me up until that moment. In fact, I had wasted four years at school going to music lessons for two hours per week and learning absolutely nothing. But looking at the Junior Corps of Drums I thought, I want to be a drummer, even though I had never played a drum in my life. The sound of the flutes and drums was exhilarating. The second point that I realised was that life isn't always fair. Our rivals, 5 Platoon, were commanded by another sergeant who was a little younger than Sgt KL. Both platoons had to do a series of marching routines and the best platoon was presented with the winning cup by the commanding officer taking the parade. Throughout the 12 weeks of basic training, I could quite clearly see that 5 Platoon were better at marching than us. The reason was that we had a couple of lads in our platoon who could not keep in step. However much Sgt KL and the two corporals pleaded, begged and threatened them with death and extra remedial marching lessons, they just couldn't keep in step with the rest of the platoon. Another reason was that 5 Platoon were just better at marching than us. It was just one of those things.

On the day of our passing out, no great surprise. Our two lads were not only consistent in getting out of step almost immediately, but managed to get the rest of the platoon out of step as well. Sgt KL was shouting, "LEFT, RIGHT, LEFT, RIGHT!" and we were marching, RIGHT, RIGHT, LEFT, LEFT. As we halted at the end of the marching routine, Sgt KL said, "Well done, lads," even though we had been a shambles and had let him down.

After this, 5 Platoon took to the stage, and we stood to attention as they went through the marching routine with perfect timing and no glitches. If it had been *Strictly Come Dancing* then they would have scored a 9 and we would have been lucky with a 3. They halted next to us and out of the corner of my eye I could see the two sergeants.

The commanding officer then stood up on the spectrum and announced the winners of the marching completion: "4 Platoon". Sgt KL marched up and accepted the winning cup on behalf of the platoon. He knew that we hadn't deserved the cup and so did the rest of us. It was a retirement present to him, as we were his last recruit platoon.

So I learnt on that day that the best team or the right team do not necessary always win. It's just life, and if you dwell on the rights and wrongs of the injustice, then it can be a handicap in your life for many years. I know, it took me a long time to accept that analogy. However, I do believe that things tend to work out in the end, if you're lucky, of course, and most of all, try and stay positive.

After the parade, I applied to Sgt KL to join the Junior Corps of Drums the next term. As he had a soft spot for the drums he allowed me to join them as a side drummer when I returned after my leave. If I had gone to 5 Platoon, their sergeant would have blocked my request because he wasn't a great lover of the Drums Platoon. Lucky I changed places with one of those lads in the queue on my first day in the Army, otherwise I'd have been in 5 Platoon.

We had two weeks' leave then I returned to the barracks. Instead of going into an Infantry platoon I went to the Drums Platoon. I spent just over a year as a junior drummer with the Corps of Drums, learning to play the side drum and bugle.

My side drumming skills were fair to average, and as I looked the part, I got away with it. But my bugle ability was renowned throughout the civilised world as simply appalling. A strangled cat would have sounded more delicate to the ears.

Looking back, the Army moulded us junior soldiers (not boy soldiers) into something worthwhile. If I had not enlisted at 16, I'm sure I would have ended up on the wrong path in life.

As a junior drummer, I performed at the various military-associated events such as the Colchester Tattoo. I also represented the Queen's Regiment as a drummer at the Royal British Legion's Remembrance Day Service at the Royal Albert Hall. It was in November 1972 and I had been a junior drummer for about six months. The service had two performances, a matinee and one in the evening. The matinee was mainly for children and families, and started around 2pm, and the evening performance started at around 7pm. This one is when the Royal family and senior dignitaries attend.

Our involvement consisted of three teams of 20 junior soldiers, negotiating a series of obstacles similar to an assault course. The fastest team to get all their men across were deemed the winners.

As junior drummers we were considered the smartest soldiers in the regiment. So there was one drummer from the Royal Anglians, one from the Royal Fusiliers, and myself representing the Queen's

Regiment. Our role was as follows.

The three drummers would each stand at the winning line and when the winning team was announced by the commentator, the sergeant major would march proudly towards the winning team's drummer and hold aloft the drummer's arm who represented the winning team. We practised and practised for many days before the race and on percentage, the Queen's team won more times than the Anglians or the Fusiliers.

So on the big day, the Royal Anglians team won the first race, the matinee performance – damn! Then the Queen's team won the evening race when The Queen, the Royal family and the VIPs were there. So the sergeant major marched up to me, held my arm aloft, and proudly shouted, "The winning team, the Queen's Regiment!" A big cheer went up from the thousands in the audience. I'm sure people thought it a fix, but it wasn't. I was a very proud boy that day.

Many years later, after a career in the Army, I attended the funeral of a lady called Mrs Spicer. She was a neighbour of ours when I lived in Greenford and she had a heart of gold. She would regularly look after all the children in the local vicinity while the mums went out to work. Almost akin to a saint. There were dozens of people of my age who attended the funeral service: all of us had been looked after by Mrs Spicer as children at one time or another. At the wake, which was held in the local church, an elderly lady, a very close friend of the shortly departed Mrs Spicer's, came up to me and asked if I was Robert Brewer. I replied that I was. She touched me gently on the arm and whispered to me that I was the only one of her children that Mrs Spicer had concerns with when I was growing up. She worried that I'd get involved with the wrong crowd and get into trouble. The elderly lady also said that Mrs Spicer was so proud of me, how I'd turned out in life and how I became a credit to my mum. I nearly welled up there and then. Occasionally it's good to clear the old tear ducts: not only does it cleanse the eyes, it also reinforces the fact that you are a human being after all.

I left Bassingbourn Barracks behind on a grey, drizzly April morning in 1973, and found myself with six other young soldiers flying out of Brize Norton military airport and arriving in RAF Gütersloh, West Germany, to join our regiment: the 2nd Battalion. The Queen's Regiment, aka 2 Queen's, aka The Buffs, who were our forefathers, were on exercise (War Games) when we arrived at the barracks. We were thrown in as Rear Party Platoon for two weeks and this consisted of guard duty, eating, drinking and sleeping. When the battalion returned I joined the 2 Battalion The Queen's Regimental Corps of Drums, considered by many to be one of the best Corps of Drums in the British Army at the time. I remained a drummer for a little over five years and had some truly memorable moments and met some great mates whom I'm still in touch with to this day, 40 years on.

One guy I met during my time as a drummer is still one of my closest friends today. We meet up once every ten years or so and reminisce about the old days, boring our wives in the process.

I served in Werl (pronounced 'Verl') in Germany for two years and met my first proper girlfriend, my first love, really. Germany was a great country for any young lad and I have lots of really happy memories.

CHAPTER 4

Prior to any tour in the province of Northern Ireland, we would get training for the 'Troubles' in a training establishment called 'Tin Town'. They were mock villages and there was one such training establishment in West Germany, where we were stationed, and another situated in the UK. The Tin Towns were made to represent the streets of N. Ireland and 1973 the training was so bloody, with no quarter given or expected. The result of this was that we inflicted more injuries on our fellow soldiers, our colleagues, during the training scenarios than were suffered at the hands of the Provisional IRA.

The battalion were posted to Londonderry (Free Derry), Northern Ireland, in November 1973. As I was still only 17 at the time, I remained in Werl and was assigned to Rear Party again for about a month. Then two days after my 18th birthday I joined my platoon at Piggery Ridge Base Camp on the outskirts of the Creggan Housing Estate in Londonderry (or Derry, depending on whose side you were on, Loyalist or Nationalist.)

The camp held two companies and an assortment of strategic staff, so in total around 250 soldiers of varying ranks. It was built on the Sheriff's Mountain and overlooked Creggan Heights, part of the notorious Creggan Estate, a constant flashpoint.

The Creggan was like one of those lawless places that you see in the old Wild West movies, a sprawl of council houses, 100% Catholic, and almost the same percentage Nationalist, and most of them hated the British Army. It was synonymous with the Bogside, which was situated a few miles away. In time I got to know the streets of the Creggan better than I knew the streets in my own neighbourhood where I grew up.

At the time, the Camp's claim to fame was that it had the biggest sandbag wall in the country, which propped up one side of the camp. The side that faced the Creggan Estate.

The reason for the sandbag wall was because the camp was constantly being attacked by the Provisional IRA with mortar fire coming from Creggan Heights a few hundred yards away. Our barrack block (sleeping quarters) was directly next to the sandbank wall.

I grew up very quickly as the 'new boy'. I was always 'Tail-End Charlie' and had to be alert and worked twice as hard as the rest of the patrol. The 'Tail-End Charlie', as the name implies, means you are at the rear of the patrol and have to learn to walk backwards. Many a lamp-post was collided into by the Tail-End Charlie of each patrol – the reason being that a sniper is not averse to shooting someone in the back or the front, it didn't really matter. The sniper didn't have the morals of John Wayne, who apparently said, "I don't shoot anyone in the back."

It was quite an eye-opener for me on my first tour to the province. I got through it without too much trouble. The mundane routine consisted of one day foot patrol, where we patrolled the Creggan Estate in two seven-man patrols, running parallel with each other. A further two mobile patrols (four vehicles, each vehicle would have either three or four soldiers) would patrol around the two foot patrols. So a total of 28 soldiers. Each patrol would last approximately two hours, after which we would all tactically return to our base. Sometimes nothing happened, and sometimes we were bricked, petrol-bombed and occasionally shot at. During the course of one day, you would probably do four to six patrols, and in between patrols it was routine to sleep (kip, gonk) and eat. The cookhouse was always open so you could eat whenever you wanted to and get yourself a hot cup of tea. The next day you would be on guard duty, which normally consisted of 'staging on' for two hours, then you'd get two hours off, then back on stag for another two hours, then two off. This would be the routine for the day. The next day would be mobile patrol, doing exactly what we did two days previously, only instead of patrolling on foot you would patrol in a vehicle. The next day we would be on quick reaction platoon, going to support any patrols that needed assistance in the city.

We would also act as admin patrol, carrying and fetching anything or anyone that needed to be transported to a certain location. Then you'd get a day off. A few beers (two was the maximum), get your dobby (laundry) done and generally chill out. Then we would start the cycle again.

I completed my first tour of N. Ireland and I don't think the regiment suffered any fatalities. As an 18-year-old, you grew up very quickly in the Army and this transition is accelerated when serving during the 'Troubles' of the early 70s in the province of Northern Ireland.

We went back to Werl after our tour had finished in March 1974 and I learnt to drive a Land Rover and gained a full German and English driving licence at the same time. I was also taught how to drive an APC (armoured personnel carrier). It's like a mini-tank but without the turret/big gun. The APC was designed to carry a section of men, 8-10, quickly over vast distances. Of course over there they drove on the right side of the road, which was natural to me at the time. I found it strange when I returned to the UK and had to drive on the left-hand side of the road for the first time.

During my time in Germany, the Drums Platoon would appear and play at many festivals called shooting festivals or in Deutschland, Schützenfests. The Germans loved these occasions and loved the British Army's Corps of Drums. Our role was to make a good impression on the civilian public, like a PR exercise. Only in those days it wasn't called PR, it was called a KAPE Tour. The KAPE mnemonic being 'Keeping the Army in the Public Eye'. So basically we would literally drive to a festival (God knows how we knew where they were), park up, get out our drums, bugles and flutes, and then join the parade.

The great thing about these festivals was that the Germans loved their beer and would provide vast amounts of German Bier while we marched. The inevitable always happened: everyone got drunk. They also loved their bands, and the music provided a really wonderful atmosphere. These festivals would last all day, and were regularly held from June to August.

We served in Werl for a further year, then the battalion was posted to Bulford in Wiltshire in late-1975. Bulford was a transit garrison with several various units of Infantry, Artillery and Engineers. I was taught to drive a Heavy Goods Vehicle (HGV3) whilst there. Having this licence helped me find work as a driver on several occasions in later years.

We went to Belize in Central America (a Commonwealth country) in early 1976 for a six-month tour. The neighbouring country, Guatemala, were threatening a war with Belize over a long-forgotten land disagreement. So the British Army sent a battalion of Infantry soldiers to help protect the country, together with an RAF squadron of Harrier Jump Jets/fighter jets. The country was mostly jungle especially 'up north', and our jungle fighting skills were harnessed and sharpened in the bars of downtown Belize City.

The Drums Platoon were stationed at Airport Camp, which was situated about 10 miles from Belize City. The rest of the battalion were spread out at two other locations, Salamanca Camp and Holdfast Camp. In the Army, if a soldier wanted to get married, he had to get permission from his commanding officer (CO). It was a rule going back to Wellington's time and normally a formality. However, any soldier requesting to see the CO regarding marriage in Belize was promptly posted 'up north' in the jungle for two months. I think a couple of soldiers married Belize girls, but not many. There were rumours that a few soldiers discharged themselves from the Army and stayed in Belize with local girls. I had my first 'near death' experience whilst serving in Belize.

I was lucky to have received scuba-diving lessons at Airport Camp which had a swimming pool, and I must have spent five weeks in total doing nothing but diving.

The British Army had the use of a small island called St. George's Caye, a few miles off the mainland, and it was used as a water sports base where we indulged in canoeing, sailing and diving. I was quite an experienced diver after the fourth week and quite confident in my ability. There was a Royal Engineer sergeant with us, and he was our main instructor.

About six of us would go out in a small boat, and the skipper, who knew the waters, would take us to the best spots for a dive. I had checked my diving gear, like you do before each dive, but I must have become complacent, because after we dived to a depth of about 25 feet, my air tube came away from my mouthpiece. Luckily I saw what had happened, otherwise I would have taken a mouthful of salt water, as opposed to air.

If this had happened, I would have started to cough and choke 25 feet underwater. Even luckier for me, the Engineer sergeant was only a few yards from me, saw what happened, and swam over to me. I was about to go into panic mode, as I had no air in my lungs. The training prior to the dives all those weeks ago paid off, because we both safely ascended to the surface using the buddy-buddy system. He would take a breath from his mouthpiece then pass it to me for my turn. He really calmed me down, because all I wanted to do was to reach the surface as quickly as possible. This would have caused me to get decompression sickness (the bends) a condition which affects your balance and hearing. When we were safely back in the boat he said to me that I had to get straight back into the sea and do another dive, otherwise "You'll bottle it and never dive again." . So after checking my kit, including the mouthpiece, the air hose and the attachment, we both got back into the sea and joined the rest of the dive team. I am eternally grateful for that Engineer sergeant. Nowadays, I would have needed counselling for months, sued the Army for thousands, and got discharged.

I recall going on an exercise for a week with ten other poor sods, to sharpen our 'survival skills'. It was the first course of its kind and we were the 'chosen few'. We were supposed to have been taken to an uninhabited island off the main coast and learned to survive by living off the land.

We had emergency rations in case we got hungry, but other than that, the aim was for us to survive off the land. We had a shotgun and cartridges and a longwave radio in case of an emergency.

So we were loaded onto this little plane which looked like a death trap. The width of the plane allowed for one person to crouch behind the person in front of them and one person behind, and so on. The seat belts were non-existent and it was really scary. So off we took and after about 15 minutes in this rust bucket, we began our descent and we could see the island below us. As we approached the airstrip, and I use the word 'airstrip' in its broadest term, we landed in the centre of a small town. It was supposed to have been an uninhabited island and yet we had landed in the middle of this shanty-like town's high street. I was amazed. What was becoming even more incredibly surreal was that the locals were having some sort of festival. This amounted to people running around with paint on their hands and smacking each other, which meant we were faced with non-hostile natives having painted faces and painted hands.

After confirming with the pilot (who only spoke Spanish) to make sure he picked us up in a week, we were then smacked in the face by locals with painted hands. We saw the plane take off and realised that someone rang a bell when a plane approached or took off. This warned the locals to stay off the street while the plane carried out its landing or take-off.

The locals were really friendly and put us up in their homes for a week. We gave them money and our rations and they fed us for the duration of our stay. We all had a great experience, spending time with these lovely native people. I think they were Aztec/Mayan-type native people who all spoke a little English. We let them have a play with the shotgun, gave them items of our uniform, and they really took care of us. After the week was up, the plane arrived (same one, same pilot) and took us back to the mainland. On our return, we each received a 'survival' certificate and were congratulated by the senior ranks for 'surviving' in the jungle for a week. No one could understand why any of us didn't look undernourished. In fact, I think I put on a couple of pounds in weight. All of us vowed to keep the experience a secret, as someone somewhere had got their wires crossed by sending us to the wrong island.

The weather was sweltering for the first four months and everybody had an all-over suntan; then came the rainy season. It rained so hard we were confined to barracks for days at a time. By the time we returned to the UK, everyone had lost their tans and the UK had experienced a mini-heatwave that year of July 1976.

We went back to Bulford for a short period, then in February 1977 we went to N. Ireland again for my second tour in the province. This time it was West Belfast, and we were stationed at Glassmullan Camp. We were Support Company, which comprised the Drums Platoon (the Bummers), the Anti-Tank Platoon (the Anti-Wanks) and the Mortar Platoon (the Drop Shorts). We spent four months exchanging bullets, both rubber and real, with the local population who enjoyed throwing bricks and petrol bombs at us on a regular basis. We didn't have it too bad where we were stationed, as Charlie Company had 'Turf Lodge'.

In 1977, this tiny estate in West Belfast was so volatile with shootings and riots on a daily basis that a patrol consisting of 100 soldiers – yes, 100 – would patrol the estate for approximately 30 minutes twice a day. There would be a number of RUC officers (the Royal Ulster Constabulary; now the PSNI, Police Service of Northern Ireland) with us as well. There would also be another 100 soldiers on the outskirts of the estate on standby, ready to go in if the first 100 got into difficulties. Virtually every day there was a riot or a shooting in Turf Lodge. You had to witness the madness to believe it. To put it into perspective, we patrolled the Glassmullan Estate regularly with an eight-man foot patrol divided into two teams of four men. We would also have a mobile patrol of two armoured Land Rovers in support which consisted of another eight men in close proximity patrolling in a parallel position to the foot patrol. Each team was able to respond to the other if either came into contact (came under fire): a total of 16 men compared with the 100 at Turf Lodge.

I got promoted to lance corporal (Lance Jack) near to the end of this tour.

Years later, I was asked, "Why does the Army have so many slang words?" Like the other two services, the Royal Navy and the RAF, the Army has a unique language understood only by those who were privileged to have served. The answer is because the Army dates back hundreds of years and many words and sayings have been grouped together from the four corners of the world, and Army language has evolved over centuries. The recipient still didn't understand my answer. Maybe that's why the Army is so unique, with a camaraderie that is unlike any other profession or institution – even marriage?

We returned to Bulford in the early summer of 77 again without any fatalities or serious injuries. Shortly afterwards we were given a three-week leave pass.

My mum passed away in October 2012 and like most people of her generation, she was a hoarder. When I went through her personal possessions after the funeral, I came across a dozen or so old postcards that I had sent her years previously from each new posting I had served at.

No telecommunications in those days, we had to rely on Her Majesty's Postal Service. So I was reading my old postcards that I had sent to my mum whenever I got a new posting. The spelling was atrocious, and each brief message contained the same: "Hi, Mum, we're in such-and-such a place, see you in such-and-such time. Rob xx." But I remember not telling my mum that I was off to Belfast in 77. When I got my three weeks' leave after our recent tour and returned home, I told a white lie and said I'd been stationed in Bulford all the time. I didn't tell her I'd been in Belfast as I know she would have been worried sick.

We arrived in Gibraltar (GIB) in the late-summer of 77. Support Company were stationed at Lathbury Barracks, which was halfway up 'The Rock'. I was only there for approximately one year, but condensed a lot into a short period. The border with Spain was closed then, so there was nowhere to go other than downtown. GIB had over 300 bars and the unofficial challenge was to get a drink in all of them during your tour. I think we managed about 30. It was a great place then with memorable stories. I met my first wife there and we would eventually get married in the main cathedral in 1979.

After a year in GIB, I was totally bored with the drums and the constant ceremonial parades. A mate of mine who had been in the Drums previously had joined the Army Dog Unit and wrote and told me how good it was. Although I was engaged at the time I just had to do something different. So I made some enquiries and decided to become a dog handler in Northern Ireland.

With a nursery lady at Stanhope
Nursery, Greenford 1957/58

4th Greenford Boy Scout
Troop (Buffalo Patrol)
1965/66

My section, Bassingbourn Barracks 1974, I've
got the 84mm Carl Gustav anti-tank weapon.

The infamous sand bag wall, Piggery Ridge Base Camp, Londonderry. With Tom, Alan and Ollie. I learnt a great deal from these veterans. Londonderry 1974

In my drums kit with my fellow drummers on a parade in Germany 1974/75

Posing with Knibbo in the APC (armoured personnel carrier) Werl 1974/75

Checking that damn air hose and mouth piece, prior to a dive. Belize 1976

*In my jungle fighting out-fit, getting in training ready for the bars
down-town Belize 1976*

Getting ready for a night patrol, West Belfast 1977

Chapter 5

So I started my training to become a dog handler with Army Dog Unit (ADU) at the Royal Army Veterinary Corps at Melton Mowbray in late-78. The unit was one of the smallest in the British Army and mainly served in Northern Ireland. There were guard dog handlers who helped to guard terrorist prisoners primarily in prison at Long Kesh, formerly the Maze Prison. They also had arms explosive dogs who searched for arms and explosives, and tracker dogs, whose call sign was 'Groundhog'. These tracked terrorists after a shooting incident.

My first training dog was called Wizz. He was a German Shepherd and a monster. After the completion of the two-week Basic Guard Dog course I got posted back to GIB for a short period. During this time I worked briefly as a dog handler working with the RAF, guarding the border between GIB and Spain. My dog at the time was a bitch (the RAF, unlike the Army, had bitches) called Nina, another GS. She was a lovely little dog with a heart of gold and I had her for brief time, then I received my posting orders and was posted to Long Kesh (the Kesh) Prison in Northern Ireland.

My first dog at the Kesh was called Rebel, and he was one of approximately 60 guard dogs, all German Shepherds, based at the prison. Rebel by name and rebel by nature, he was a headstrong dog and needed a lot of encouragement to do as he was told.

The Army helped the Prison Service in guarding some of the most violent terrorists (or freedom fighters, depending on whose side you were on) and non-terrorists in the country.

The Army guarded paramilitaries of both persuasions. On the Republican side, you had the Provisional Irish Republican Army (Provos) and INLA, the Irish National Liberation Army, and on the Loyalist side, the UFF, the Ulster Freedom Fighters, who were part of the UDA. I was there when the Republican prisoners were on their dirty protest, but the Army were not directly involved with the protesters: that was the sole remit of the Prison Service.

The guard dog handler's shift pattern consisted of one day on and one day off. On your day on, you'd start at 7am, feed your dog, then get your patrol duties from the senior corporals. There would be six dog handlers per shift, and we had our designated patrol routes. The Prison Service, with their guard dogs, patrolled at the same time as us, but at different locations. After the two-hour patrol, we would get two hours off, then back on patrol for another two hours, and so on for the next 24 hours. We would finish at 7am the next day, which would then be the start of our rest day.

The routine then would be to feed Rebel, then a little exercise for him, then breakfast for us. We would then get some kip, have a shower and then head into town for a drink or three. The town was Lisburn, which was relatively safe from Provo attacks, although the town did suffer a few atrocities over the years.

Long Kesh was the main prison, but occasionally we would also provide guard dogs at Magilligan Prison which was near Limavady, County Londonderry. It was a one-week posting after which we would go back to the Kesh. After four months of guard dog duties, I applied, and was accepted, to be a specialist dog handler. I had about two weeks to go before my three-month Tracker Handler's Course when I got a posting to Magilligan Prison. It was a very laid-back posting and the dog handlers went on patrol almost on an ad hoc basis. It was late-January and I had been there for a couple of days when I took Rebel out for some exercise. The countryside next to the prison was beautiful and the view overlooked the Irish Republic which was separated by a thin strip of sea. There was a beach and in January there were very few tourists.

On this particular occasion, I had let Rebel off his lead and let him roam free. I took my eye off him for a matter of seconds to take in the scenery when all of a sudden the little bugger bolted.

I screamed, "Rebel!" but he totally ignored me, having spotted some sheep, and off he went into the distant yonder. I ran after him, but lost sight of him: he was off. I must have been looking for him for a couple of hours. I didn't tell my colleagues back at the base, as we both would have been in trouble. I had visions of Rebel finding his way across the water and running amok in the Irish Republic.

Eventually after shouting myself hoarse, I saw a little head peering from behind a great lump of grass. I ran up to him and gave him the biggest punch to his jaw. It hurt me more than it hurt him. (He was a prison guard dog and was as hard as nails.) I made him walk to heel all the way back to the prison, about two miles away. When we eventually got back, I opened his kennel and shouted at him to get in. No dinner for him. I got back to the barrack boom, no one noticed that I had been gone for about three hours, such was the laid-back environment, luckily for me. After about 20 minutes, I thought I'd better go and check on him (guilt had set in, maybe). So I went to the kennels, a short distance from our barrack room. There were four other guard dogs in the compound: each dog had its own run and kennel which was separated from the other dogs by a metal chain-link fence. To get into the compound, you had to go through a series of metal gates, then you would arrive at your dog's own gate.

Now the dogs could hear you when you approached and were all up and barking in their own kennels. Usually Rebel was the first up to his own gate, and would probably bark the loudest.

But on this occasion I could see four of the dogs up barking to their own compound, but I couldn't see Rebel. F@@k, I thought, what's happened to him? I called out his name, and almost immediately he came bounding out of his kennel, barking like all of the other dogs. He had literally been 'in the doghouse'. When he heard my calming voice and knew I wasn't angry with him anymore he was back to his old mischievous self. At the time I was angry with him, but in hindsight it was my fault, because after all, he was only the dog and I was the dog handler.

I started my Specialist Dog Handler Course shortly after this episode (someone else took on Rebel: lucky them) and I was posted back to Melton Mowbray for a 3-month course as a tracker dog handler. My initial tracker dog was called Tex. He was another German Shepherd and a very good tracker. Unfortunately, Tex had a habit of biting people. So to send him back to Northern Ireland would not have been a sensible idea. The reason being that specialist dog handlers were often flown into a hot spot (an area where a shooting or other similar incident had recently happened) in a helicopter and, as Tex was quite volatile, it was feared that he might have a go at the helicopter crew, which would not have been too good.

So after four weeks with Tex, I was given another tracker dog, named Lotus. He was a black Labrador and one of the best tracker dogs the Army Veterinary Corps had. I hasten to add that the Corps were responsible for the training of dogs and their handlers, and were considered to have some of the best trainers in the world.

So I bonded with Lotus for the next eight weeks learning how to track and read Lotus's signs, i.e. when he was on track and when he was faking it. It's said that a dog's sense of smell is ten times greater than a human's and that everybody gives off a different scent. It's called a scent picture and we've all got a different one individual to each person, like a set of fingerprints.

So after completing three months of training, I returned to the province of N. Ireland with Lotus as a specialist tracker dog handler. I was initially posted to 3 Brigade which was unofficially considered to be the busiest of the three brigades in the province. Its area of operation was the counties of Fermanagh, Tyrone and Armagh. The other two brigades were 39 Brigade, which covered Belfast and the surrounding areas, and 8 Brigade which covered Londonderry and Mid Ulster. I was stationed at North Armagh Barracks.

Due to the dangers of improvised explosive devices (IEDs) hidden by the side of the road, Lotus and I travelled everywhere in a helicopter. It was usually either a Westland Scout (just called Scout) or the slightly larger Gazelle. Both helicopters had just enough room for the pilot, the co-pilot, Lotus and myself. We would land near the hot spot where the shooting had taken place and Lotus would do his work in tracking the scent of the gunmen. He was on an 18-foot pilot line, so if he accidentally activated a booby trap he would suffer the full force of the blast and I would be relatively unscathed. I was never comfortable with this scenario, as dog handlers formed strong bonds with their dogs.

We had many successful encounters during our time with 3 Brigade. The terrorists/freedom fighters had a sliding scale for killing SF (security forces), and specialist dog handlers were high up on the list. I spent five months in 3 Brigade and loved every minute.

I got married for the first time in 1979 and as it was considered to be too dangerous to work in 3 Brigade as a married man, I was posted to 8 Brigade and stationed in Londonderry. We lived in the married quarters, which was considered to be in a relatively safe area in the city and not far from the barracks.

I was posted to 8 Brigade as a specialist dog handler for approximately 15 months and had some fantastic times and made some very good mates. The soldiers of Army Dog Unit were a special breed – forgive the pun. As an arms explosive dog handler or a tracker dog handler, pitting your skills against those of a formidable adversary was always a challenge. Most of the handlers were from the Paras, Royal Marine Artillery, Royal Engineers or elite Infantry regiments.

So my life at the time consisted of one day on duty, then one day off. This routine lasted for four weeks, after which I was stationed for two weeks in Mid Ulster. Initially I tracked for the Royal Marine Commandos, then after about a year it was with the Grenadier Guards. So as you can imagine, my wife very rarely saw me.

Lotus and I did some good tracks, and I always thought that he was the aeroplane and I was the pilot. He was an easy dog to read (reading your dog was essential: you had to know when he was on track and when he had lost the scent) and so this made tracking quite enjoyable.

The dogs of the Army Dog Unit would get a holiday once a year and one year we went to Comrie, Crieff, in Perthshire, Scotland. We stayed in an old Army barracks, and half the unit would go for a week, then we would change over, and the other half would have their holiday. The logistics of this holiday were off the scale. The Army had to get approximately 50 dogs, guard dogs, arms explosive (A&E) dogs and tracker (Groundhog) dogs, together with their handlers, on the ferry from Belfast to Stranraer in Scotland. Then we would be driven in Army vehicles the 100-plus miles to the barracks in Comrie. A truly remarkable logistical feat. We went there in June, and the countryside was truly stunning. At that time of year, the colours that come off the glens are truly remarkable.

The idea was to let the dogs, especially the German Shepherds, have a really good time, running loose in the countryside. After all, they deserved a well-earned break from their normal tasks of guarding the prisons in Northern Ireland. As for the specialist dogs, A&E and the Groundhogs, we were given plenty of training scenarios to complete.

About halfway through our week's holiday, Lotus and I were given the task to track three men, who were our trainers from the Army Veterinary Corps. This track was to be over three miles and through the Perthshire countryside. The extra pressure on us was that all of the other 50 dogs and dog handlers would be following us. They started about 100 yards behind Lotus and me and in a single file stretching back some distance. The sight must have been a wonderment; sadly I didn't see it, because I was concentrating on reading Lotus and making sure he was still on track. If we had a balls-up and got everybody lost, then there would have been 50 or so very angry dog handlers. I don't think the dogs would have been too worried, as they were all on a jolly. So after about two hours of tracking, we finally tracked our prey hiding in a large tuft of grass in a glen. Well done, Lotus: he was the star of the day.

It was normally a two-year posting with the ADU and after my time was up, I decided to return to my regiment who were stationed in Colchester, Essex. I had heard a rumour that the regiment were off to

Hong Kong for two years, so naturally I jumped at the chance.

My first child, a son, was conceived around this time.

As Lotus was past his best and due for a well-deserved retirement, the ADU allowed me to take him with me. So I had a new wife and an old dog when I returned to the regiment.

When I left the ADU, I was a full corporal, but when I arrived back with the regiment I was reduced in the ranks to a private again. I decided not to return to the Corps of Drums, and instead went to a Rifle Company. As I hadn't done any serious Infantry work since I was in basic training, it was a bit of a shock to the system. I was also in my mid- to late-twenties, and all the other private soldiers were about five years younger than me.

CHAPTER 6

I ended up in 7 Platoon, B Company (B Coy), and spent a further five years with them. Like the Corps of Drums, I made some great friends. I was somewhat of a novelty because I became a sergeant within five years, which was some going, especially as I had no idea what I was doing when I first joined B Coy.

In the space of four years, I completed a Junior Non-Commissioned Officers course, a Skill at Arms Instructors Course, a Senior Brecon, a course for Sergeants, and I took the Educational Promotional Certificate Advanced (EPCA), which was a mandatory educational qualification for sergeants to take and pass for promotion to a warrant officer. The educational qualification consisted of four subjects: English, Maths, Man Management, and The Army in the Contemporary World.

But I'm jumping ahead of myself. In 1980, after a few months in Colchester it became apparent that we were not going to go to Hong Kong as I initially thought. I got promoted to lance corporal in 1981 after a year as a private. We managed to get a posting to Cyprus for six months. Three months in Dhkelia, a Sovereign Base Area in the south-east of the country, and three months on the United Nations Line keeping the Greeks and Turks apart. During this time I did my Skill at Arms Instructors Course at the home of Infantry Training, Warminster, in Wiltshire. It was a nine-week course which would enable me to teach every single military Infantry weapon in the British Army.

After completing the course I would be part of the elite instructors in the Army. I then joined my platoon in Cyprus who had already been stationed there for about a month.

I was awarded the United Nations (UN) Medal to add to my General Service Medal that was awarded to me for serving in N. Ireland. During my time in Cyprus, I joined the Battalion's Shooting Team, and spent a large proportion of my time in Cyprus on the shooting ranges.

The regiment won through the preliminary stages and went on to Bisley, the British Army's shooting competition, which is held each year and lasts for about two weeks. I managed to be on the shooting team, and went back to Bisley for a further two more years.

During my stint on the shooting team, I managed to win a couple of medals and cups for shooting a variety of weapons in a number of shooting competitions. I was lucky because I was more of a reliable team shot, as opposed to a really good individual marksman.

In 1983, I was posted back to Northern Ireland and once again it was Londonderry for another two-year stint. My first wife managed a month, after which, by mutual agreement, we parted company. We had been married for three years, but were only probably together for ten months.

For the next two years I experienced a number of incidents involving the army, my fellow soldiers and the Provisional IRA. As it was a two-year posting, the rota was a little easier than a straightforward four-month tour where you are almost working flat out for the duration. With a two-year posting it went like this:

First month: operations.

Next month: training.

Next month: operations again.

Then the last month in the four-month cycle was Leave and Adventure Training.

So the two years went quite quickly and weren't too bad.

I ended up as acting platoon sergeant and managed to bring my platoon home all in one piece – well, physically anyway. I was involved in a number of war stories yet again, but one really stands out and sent a shiver down my back when I first heard of it a number of years later.

Jump forward 30 years and you are in a totally different world regarding communication, computers etc. In early 2015, I was browsing on Facebook and a picture caught my eye. It was of a young soldier on the streets of Northern Ireland. I remember the soldier and even recognised the location.

Through curiosity I started reading the summary and realised it was about me. To keep this short, this soldier had posted that pic on FB at the end of October 2014, 30 years after the event he was recalling. It was Halloween night in Londonderry: he was under fire from a gunman, and nearly ended up shooting me or someone else in my section. When I first read it, I felt a shiver down my back. Being killed by friendly fire is the 'in phrase' now, for being shot and killed by your own side. I immediately contacted the ex-soldier through Facebook and he relayed the story to me again in more detail. It turned out that he was a split second away from shooting me dead, having realised his mistake in the nick of time – luckily for me.

This is the account of the night in question as written on FB by my fellow soldier.

"Halloween, thirty years ago today I was sitting in the back of a Land Rover going down Central Drive in the Creggan (Londonderry). Bob Hammond was commanding, Mark Lygo was driving, and Colin Marquette was on top cover. We were the second wagon, the front one was commanded by Steve Arthey. We were on our way back from a patrol in the Creggan, heading back to RUC Rosemount. As we passed the school we drew level with a foot patrol led by Bob Brewer.

All of a sudden CRACK-THUMP, CRACK-THUMP (followed by five more, but you get the gist). (We're being shot at.) We de-bus and go into cover trying to locate the firing point.

Being the junior member of the team I got to carry the IWS (the

CWS's older and bigger brother to you young ones). (A night scope.)

I start scanning into the dark looking for movement: everything is green and the sight is making that strange winging nose (like a mosquito in flight). Looking up the street I am immediately struck by how surreal things are.

All I can see is a mass of kids done up in Halloween costumes, out doing the trick or treat thing, only now there are small groups of ghosts, witches and vampires, desperately trying to be as small as possible as they cower behind parked cars.

I hear Steve shout and turn to the left to cover into the area of the school. F**k, there's the gunman. I see him running away from me with rifle in his hand, F**K ME!!! My first contact and I'm going to kill a terrorist, I'm in autopilot, safety catch is off, steady my breathing, sight aligned, my finger takes up the first pressure.

I am just about to kill a man and the dreadful realisation hits me, that my target is not a member of the PIRA, but Bob Brewer and his team, in hot pursuit, going for the firing point. The safety catch is back on and I break out in a cold sweat. My first contact I nearly kill one of my own platoon.

That was the start of a very busy month in the city (The Bn's last) and we had several more contacts, and I'm very pleased I did not have any more such near misses. I didn't have the bottle to tell Bob what happened until the next month. By now we had left Northern Ireland and were in our new home, Oakington near Cambridge. The whole platoon was out on the piss in Monroe's (a bar in Cambridge). I finally plucked up the courage to tell him: the response was not what I expected, and I was half-expecting to get punched. But Bob just looked at me and said, 'Glad you didn't fire, now get the beers in.'

30 years ago, where did that go? To all those lads of 7 Pl (Well-ards) wherever you are, I hope you are well."

Wow. Lucky me!!

One other incident always saddens me. We were coming to the end of our two-year posting. I think we had less than ten days to go and B Company were the last on operational duties in the city.

My patrol was on mobile patrol in the Creggan Estate, when we heard an explosion coming from the Rossville Flats in the Bogside. We were about two miles away, but drove like the devil to get there.

We were first on the scene and quickly discovered that an eight-man patrol had been ambushed in the flats, and two soldiers had very serious injuries. I recall seeing an ambulance arriving seconds before us, and as the ambulance man got out he was headbutted by a youth in the crowd. My section had to deal with this carnage until reinforcements arrived.

A group of about 20 or so in the crowd then started to throw bricks and bottles at us, and cheering the fact that a British Army patrol had been attacked. This was while we were trying to deal with our injured colleagues. I really had to rein my men in, as one or two were on a short fuse and ready to start firing live rounds (real bullets) at the crowd.

I recall seeing the ambulance man, who had earlier been assaulted, dealing with the injured while blood streamed from his nose. These people were truly unsung heroes. I think that two soldiers of the patrol that had been ambushed had received very serious injuries but thankfully not fatal.

Some years later, the Army presented me with the Accumulated Campaign Service Medal for services rendered for Queen and Country. This was achieved by serving for four more years on active duty, like in N. Ireland, Afghanistan, Iraq etc.

On a slightly lighter note, virtually everyone took sugar in their tea and coffee at the time. Any hot drink was called a NATO Standard, which meant any hot drink with two spoons of sugar. If you didn't take sugar in your tea, you had to lump it, no pun intended.

I had a particularly sweet tooth and would regularly add even more sugar to my NATO Standard tea or coffee. We had been at a small Army base location for about ten days, when the 'powers that be' received intelligence that the Provos were going to carry out a rocket attack on a mobile vehicle patrol at our location.

As our base was very small, we relied upon a replenishment (replen) of rations (food) on a regular basis, and this was by way of armoured vehicles delivering our essentials. As there was an embargo on vehicles entering and departing from our base location, the cook had to make do with what he had in the larder. Mother Hubbard springs to mind. This embargo lasted for about a week, and the first item to run out was sugar.

Our cook was commended with his concoctions of different foods that he served up to 20-plus soldiers three times a day. I think he was awarded the BEM, British Empire Medal, for his ingenuity. So after about four days without sugar, I managed to give up that particular vice. Even to this day, I dislike with a vengeance any tea or coffee that's made NATO-style.

Another notable occurrence related to the Chai Wallahs. This is probably a politically incorrect term now, but in those days it was never intended as a slur in any form. As I understand it, it means Chai, Tea, Wallah, Seller. The soldiers that served on every foreign base in the world were forever grateful for the CWs serving egg and bacon rolls, etc, hot drinks and adult mags to the troops for up to 18 hours every day of the year, including Christmas Day. We were not sure of their nationality, either Indian, Pakistani or Afghan, but their services were invaluable.

On one occasion, a Provo Active Service Unit tried to blow up Rosemount Army Base in Londonderry. They attacked the camp with small arms fire and threw petrol bombs at the sangers (watchtowers). The CWs worked hand in hand with the soldiers at the base to put out the fires in the buildings and sangers. Then, when everything was back under control, off they went to make us cups of tea and bacon sandwiches.

I met my second wife during the end of my two years in Londonderry, and went on to have two wonderful girls with her. Alas, the marriage only lasted ten years, and it was mainly my fault that it ended.

I left Northern Ireland at the end of 1984, having spent the best part of four years and four months of my adult life patrolling the various streets and rural areas of the province. The regiment was then posted to Oakhampton Barracks in Cambridge. This was an old RAF camp with a couple of airfields and was quite run-down. I did hear that it was converted into an immigration removal centre (IRC) some years later. It was a culture shock for the regiment as well as the residents of Cambridge and the surrounding areas, because we had two years of Londonderry to get out of our system.

In the early part of 1985, the Battalion was on exercise in Catterick, a dreadful place in the North of England near the Yorkshire Dales. It was the battalion's first major military exercise since returning from N. Ireland. We were there for approximately two weeks and I don't think it stopped raining once. The privates were all billeted together, and after the first week it was apparent that the ones in my platoon were up to something.

At every opportunity, the senior privates would huddle together and discuss something in hushed whispers. I was the senior corporal/acting platoon sergeant at the time and it was my job to know exactly what was going on. I soon found out that the privates were engaged in a Ouija board in their barrack room when the day's activities were over.

In the Army at the time, it was not uncommon for a Ouija board to be used as a recreational tool. Soldiers are very superstitious and had all manner of beliefs. I had heard of the Ouija board – we all had – but I had never been involved, as I was always a little anxious of what it might conjure up. There were always rumours of soldiers doing all sorts of crazy things for no obvious or apparent reason after a session on the board. Don't forget, we all had access to guns and ammunition. Not a good combination if one went a little crazy, so the consequences of a fallout could be catastrophic.

A few of the senior privates asked me and the other corporals if they could come to our room, because they were convinced they had been in contact with a spirit. They wanted us to verify it, and to convince themselves that one of their own was not inadvertently or subconsciously pushing the top. So we invited them over to the corporal's room to set up the board. I then spent approximately two hours convinced that we were in contact with a spirit.

First of all, the letters of the alphabet t A to Z, and the numbers 0 to 9, were laid next to each other to form a complete circle. Then the words 'Yes' and 'No' were placed in the middle of the circle. All of this was on our communal table that was part of the furniture in every barrack room in the British Army. To make this experience even more incredible was our top or cup. Now everyone will tell you that the top or cup has to be a glass for use on a Ouija board. Wrong. Our receptacle was a plastic cup off the top of a tin of shaving foam that most men used at the time. The room was full of soldiers, the lights were out, and we used torches with red and green filters to add to the mystical atmosphere.

As I said, initially I was very sceptical about the whole episode and didn't want to take part, but at the same time I was highly intrigued. So for the first 20 minutes I was an observer, as four of my fellow soldiers were seated at the table with their index fingers on the top of the cup. We called these 'boarders' and they went through the routine of...

"Is there anybody there?"

"Where are you from?"

"What's your name?"

"How old are you?"

"How did you die?"

And other open and close questions of a similar nature. It wasn't too exciting, as the top looked to be just moving around the board without any coherent meaning.

Then one of the four boarders decided he did not want to carry on, and I felt a strange feeling drawing me to the board. So I took his place and became the fourth boarder. Off we went, four index fingers, mine and the other three boarders, on the plastic top, which was moving around the table. We also had a scribe, one soldier, not a boarder, who tried to write down the answers given by our spirit. It didn't seem to make sense.

"How old are you?" The top moved to 2 then it moved to 3.

We then asked, "So you are 23?" The Top then moved to "*No*".

We asked its name, and we received an illegible answer of random letters. So for the first 30 minutes or so it continued to make little sense, although we were all convinced that no one was moving the top. When we asked, "When did you die?" the Top moved to *1 9 4 1*.

So we asked if it had died in the war, the reply was "*Yes*".

So we all assumed that he was a soldier and had died in the 2nd World War. So off we went:

"Are you English?" "*No*".

"Are you German?" "*No*".

We must have asked after every nationality involved in the 2nd World War. Then I asked:

"Are you from Africa?" and the Top went to "*Yes*".

Then I had an idea. I asked again for the umpteenth time:

"How old are you?" the Top again went to 2 then 3.

I then said, "Are you 23 months old?" The Top moved to "*Yes*".

"So you are a 23-month-old African baby?" It went to "*Yes*".

"So you can't spell your name because you're a baby?" "*Yes*".

"Do you have a name?" "*No*".

"So shall we call you Baby?" "*Yes*".

"Do you like the name Baby?" "*Yes*".

"You must think we are being silly." "*Yes*".

"So Baby have a play."

Baby then raced around the table with our fingers barely touching the top.

Now the thing about a barrack room table in the British Army is that it's used for everything: ironing your kit (uniform), writing letters home and making tea and coffee (making a brew). Because of this, parts of the top of the table, normally Formica, become sticky with the leftovers of tea, coffee and sugar.

Well, Baby knew to circumnavigate these sticky spots and race around the table. So for the next hour or so, we asked Baby all manner of questions. A couple of things we thought we cleared up regarding our young spirit. Firstly, we believed that he was a boy, but we weren't quite sure why. Also, when he said he died in 1941, we think it was a war between villages in Africa. If you think of this period in Africa, there were probably several inter-village/tribe battles going on, and Baby could have died in one such dispute.

After about an hour, we could feel that he was getting tired, as the top was starting to move slowly. After all, there is only so much energy the spirit of an African baby can have. We did ask if there was a Heaven and Baby replied that there was, but for some reason he wasn't there. We asked him if there was anything we could do to help him get to Heaven like praying. He replied, "*Yes*".

I then said, "On the count of three, you had better go." Baby replied, "*Yes*".

I then counted out loud:

"One"... "*Yes*".

"Two"... "*Yes*".

"Three"... Nothing! The top did not move. I felt the spirit gone. I had a sleepless night and vowed never to do that again – or maybe not. Many years later, I met an ex-soldier who recalled that evening. We spoke at length of our contact with a spirit and both of us were convinced that we had made contact with Baby. Shortly after the exercise at Catterick, I was promoted to full platoon sergeant and posted to the Army Careers Office in Acton, London, as a recruitment sergeant.

I spent the next two years living the life of Riley. During this period, I got married for the second time and we bought a small house in Milton Keynes. I would travel down each day by train to the Army Careers Office and work 9-5, Monday to Friday. I had never experienced normal working hours before and so I became what's known as 'civilianised'.

There were two other sergeants working in the Careers Office as well as myself, and we also had the office manager. He was a staff sergeant,, which is one rank up from a sergeant. Everyone in the office also worked at The Duke of York Theatre in London, as fire and security officers. The musical was *Stepping Out* and it ran for three years. There were a number of recognisable TV actresses who appeared in the musical and all of them had a pleasant disposition. At one time I was spending more time at The Duke of York Theatre than I was at the Army Careers Office.

Nearing the end of my first year, I sat an exam for promotion to warrant officer.

It's called the Educational Promotion Certificate Advanced (EPCA) and consisted of four subjects:

Maths

English

The Army in the Contemporary World (Politics)

Man Management (ManM)

By far, ManM was the hardest of the four subjects to pass. Together with 10 other sergeants, I attended Chelsea Barracks in London and studied for two months in preparation for the exams.

The teachers were all Army officers, mainly captains and lieutenants. I remember one officer acknowledge that ManM was the hardest subject to pass, but he said that if we did what he told us, and not what we thought, then we'd get through it and pass the wretched subject.

I later learnt that at least half of the sergeants on the course with me had taken their EPCA in the past, but had not managed to pass the ManM subject. I listened to what that officer had to tell me and passed all four subjects at the first attempt and gained a distinction in ManM.

I'm not sure how many young men I personally recruited into Her Majesty's Armed Forces, maybe in the region of about 50. So I am responsible for altering the lives of 50 people. I hope it was for the better, and the majority of those 50 young men got a positive return for their endeavours. I recall a handful who I honestly thought showed great promise and would go far in their respective careers. For every 10 young men who came through the door of the Army Careers Office, only one would be good enough for a career in the Army.

When I was not working evenings at the theatre, I would do voluntary work at my local youth club. In those days it was wasn't necessary to have any formal checks or training, so I became a volunteer youth leader. The only prerequisite, it seemed, was to turn up, take abuse from the children, then go home. My co-workers consisted of the manager, a very nice woman, and two youth assistants, who were also both very nice. I have learnt in life that boys and girls aged between ten and 16 generally walk all over 'nice' people.

So when Sergeant Bob Brewer arrived, being in the regular Army, the inevitable happened.

I was there for around six months, turning up most Tuesdays between 7 and 9pm, so a few things were pulled into line. No smoking if they were under 16, which most of them were. Everyone paid on the dot for their drinks and hot dogs, which meant the end of IOUs. We had no swearing and no bullying, and some of the older kids thought they owned the pool table. They soon found out from me that they didn't.

I was quite proud to meet up with some of those little yobs some years later and realised that most had turned out quite respectable. I always liked to think, correctly or otherwise, that I had a positive impact on some of those kids' lives. I know that a team from the youth club reached the regional finals of an 'It's a Knockout' competition.

As a footnote to this episode, I was in a shop in Milton Keynes in 2016, 29 years after my stint at the youth club, when I bumped into one of the original youth workers. He hadn't changed too much and we started to reminisce. Sadly, he told me shortly after I had left, the staff had trouble with disruptive behaviour and ended up closing the club.

So back to 1986. I was beginning to think seriously about my career in the Army. As I had become civilianised, the thought of going back to the regiment and doing proper Infantry work again did not appeal to me. I heard that the regiment were stationed in West Germany at the time, which meant endless months on exercise (war games) and more tours back to Belfast or Londonderry.

So after some soul-searching, I decided to hand my notice in and leave the Army. I had to give one year's notice which gave me plenty of time to reconsider my decision to quit the Army. After a soldier serves their time in the Army, they are entitled to a resettlement course. As the name implies, it's a course that enables soldiers to get a job in Civvy Street.

As I achieved a distinction in man-management, it was suggested to that I could go to college for a term and gain some qualifications in personnel management. Thus a career in personnel beckoned.

However, I had no idea what it actually entailed.

So most soldiers about to leave the Army attended useful courses such as training in how to become a plumber, decorator, electrician etc. Instead I went to Plymouth College and took courses for the National Examining Board in Supervisory Management (NEBSM Dip) and the Institute of Personnel Management (IPM) and passed them both. Except for one other person, the course was exclusively for officers in the Army, Royal Navy and the Royal Air Force. So I was a fish out of water to some degree, being only a humble platoon sergeant.

So I finished my course at the college and achieved diplomas in Personnel Management.

I completed my last few months as a sergeant in the Army at the Army Careers Office, Acton, West London. I do recall having major doubts just before I was due to leave. After all, the Army had been my life for the last 15 years, 13 years as an adult and two as a junior soldier, and I was unsure of what the future held for me.

I left the Army in September in 1987 after serving over 15 years, man and boy. I had no great send-off, just a few beers at the local pub with my fellow recruitment sergeants.

CHAPTER 7

I don't really recall my last days in the Army, but I remember thinking, why not try the police? An old friend of my mum's was an ex-police officer and he had previously served in the RAF. I met up with him and he suggested a career in the London Police Force, aka the MET.

I was living in Milton Keynes at the time and I assumed that this area was covered by the MET. Wrong. Milton Keynes in fact comes under the authority of the Thames Valley Police, a totally different police force. What did I know?

So I applied to join Thames Valley Police while still being in the Army. I ended up attending their headquarters situated in Kidlington, Oxford. There must have been around 60 applicants, a mixture of male and female of various ages, and all were white with the exception of me.

We all took the written test which consisted of five subjects: English, Maths and three other topics which were designed to test your lateral thinking. After a little while, a staff member came into the classroom and called out approximately 30 names and asked those she had read out to leave the room. My name was amongst those that had not been called out. So the other 30 of us remained where we were, not knowing if we were the successful ones or the failures. After a few more agonising moments, a staff member came back into the classroom and informed us all that we had all passed and that Thames Valley Police would be in touch with all of us in the near future.

So as I waited for the call from Thames Valley Police, I applied for various jobs. After all, I had a mortgage and bills to pay; besides, going on the dole was alien to me. I had a Heavy Goods Vehicle licence and went to a recruitment agency seeking temporary work as an HGV driver.

On my first visit to the recruitment agency, I was interviewed by the manager and she asked if I wanted to work for them as a recruitment consultant. I had no previous experience in this field but decided to give it a go. I contacted Thames Valley Police, informing them that I no longer wanted to become a police officer.

So my first full-time job since I'd become a civilian was as a recruitment consultant. I worked in an office with four women, and two other men who were the company's accountants. This was my first time working in a female-dominated office environment and it was an education.

I lasted approximately six months and then left, and worked for another recruitment agency who had headhunted me. It really boosts your ego when a competitor asks you to join their firm. This time there were only three of us in the office. I lasted slightly longer this time, about seven months. I soon realised an office environment was not for me.

I then secured a job as a sales rep, selling cable television in the local area. This lasted for about a year, then I moved on to become a deputy restaurant manager working for a well-known pizza company. I was there for about 18 months and recall having an interview with the regional manager when I put in my notice to quit. He basically offered the restaurant to me if I stayed.

During this time I was hungry to experience as much as I could in life, thinking I had somehow missed out because I'd joined the Army at such a young age.

My first daughter arrived in the world about this time of my life. It was a little traumatic because she had turned in her mum's womb and was upside down. Luckily, a quick-thinking midwife spotted it early enough and my first daughter was born through an emergency Caesarean.

I was in a bar in Milton Keynes many years later and bumped into a party of around 15 ex-members of the pizza restaurant. Apparently they all kept in touch through social media and were, in their words, "over the moon" to see me. (It does the heart good to hear that.)

It was surreal to see these guys because I remember most of them as young, gobby, spotty uni kids, and now they were all grown up with families of their own. I was humbled when they said that the training we provided in the restaurant was the best training that they had ever received. One guy, who I remember particularly well because we exchanged words on more than one occasion, had advanced in life and had gone on to own an IT business.

He said that he wouldn't have been where he was today without getting the 'life skills' taught by the management at the pizza restaurant.

After I left the restaurant business I had a variety of jobs from selling advertising space to being a bus driver in London which I thoroughly enjoyed.

Then in March 1992 I finally joined Thames Valley Police (TVP) and was stationed at Central Milton Keynes Police Station. Now every police officer has to do their two years as a probationary police officer (Proby). During this time we would learn all the basics of being a good copper. That meant lots of drinking, socialising and trying not to get kicked off the police force.

The two years went something like this:
A. One week at Sulhamstead (Sully) (TVP's training school).
B. Ten weeks at Ashford (another training school) completing various training modules.
C. Five weeks on shift with my tutor constable (good bloke) who spent all his time telling me to forget all that I had learnt at Ashford, because it didn't equate to the real world.
D. Five weeks back at Ashford, completing more training modules.
E. Five further weeks with my tutor constable, again telling me to forget the last five weeks, as it was all pretty meaningless.
F. Two weeks' CID attachment (see further on).
G. Two weeks' traffic attachment (see further on).
H. One week Coroner's Office attachment (pretty spooky, had to watch

an autopsy).

I. One week with the admin ladies at the police station who told us how they wanted the paperwork completed.

2. J. Two weeks' Post-Foundation Course (PF1) held at Sully. This was designed to iron out any bad habits that we had picked up while being on shift in the real world.

K. Back on shift, and ignoring what the instructors had told us on PF1. (This was repeated on two more occasions, as we did PF2 and PF3, again, both for two weeks and both at Sully.)

L. Then back on shift, ignoring everything that we had been taught on PF2 and PF3.

In between all the courses you went on patrol like any regular copper with an experienced police officer. After about 16 months the sergeants knew whether or not we were going to make it. After finally completing all of the attachments, all of the modules and all of the training, and you hadn't made a major cock-up, you were told that you had successfully completed your two-year probation.

That's it in a nutshell, now for a little more meat:

My first week as a police officer was an induction training course at the Forces Training Centre at Sulhamstead (Sully) which was just outside Reading in Berkshire.

We were the infamous 'Course of 3/92'.

There were about 40 of us and about a third of us were ex-military. Also most of the intake were in their thirties and had some life skills.

There were many memorable moments during my first week as a copper, but one sticks in my mind the most. In those days it wasn't frowned upon to have a few drinks after work and let your hair down.

During a session in the bar at Sully one evening, about 30 police officers in a rather merry state embarked on a rough 'n' tumble game of indoor rugby at the training centre's bar. There were no civilians involved, just police officers. It was all very harmless, and during the game we all started singing the rugby song, "Swing Low, Sweet Chariot", all good fun.

The next day, I was summoned into the training commander's office. I thought, 'F@@k me.' I wasn't the only one having a rough 'n' tumble. Imagine my astonishment when I was asked if I felt offended in any way due to the singing of a slave song. 'Political correctness' had started to creep in back in 1992.

After my initial induction training, I went to Ashford for the next ten weeks to complete my training modules (I think there were 68 core responsibilities that made up the training modules, and you had to pass each one). The basic training at Ashford was really a free-for-all. I was married at the time and took my wedding vows seriously, unlike a large percentage of my fellow coppers, both male and female.

The training itself consisted of getting drunk most nights and trying to stay awake for the endless laborious training modules.

The training in most part was virtually a waste of time. This was because it consisted of 'role play'-type scenarios, and didn't bear any resemblance to real-life situations. Seasoned officers always said after you'd competed your training modules, your actual training would start on the streets with real-life scenarios.

The three PF courses held at Sully were renamed Pint Fondling 1, Pint Fondling 2, and Pint Fondling 3, because there was such a total lack of any coherent or meaningful training and was more about hitting the bars at night.

So the training became one big joke. Even more remarkable were my final marks on my PDR (Personnel Development Report): 'Well above average' and just off from being 'outstanding'. Unbelievable really. I should have gone to the pub even more, then maybe I would have achieved that 'outstanding' mark.

I completed my two years' probation, and for the next 18 years and ten months I was a good, old-fashioned copper with Thames Valley's finest. And for the first four years it was easy. Going out on patrol, nicking people, putting them in front of the custody sergeant, a quick pocket notebook entry (PNB), then back out on patrol and looking for more bad people to arrest. A great job.

In the early to mid-90s our bread and butter criminals were, in no particular order: burglars, car thieves, aggressors involving domestic violence (DV), and good, old-fashioned public order. It was an easy job and I was on a good shift with good sergeants. Some memorable moments were:

Arresting my first offender, a person who had an illegal tax disc displayed in his car.

It was my first arrest and interview: every police officer remembers their first arrest. You've passed your probation and your sergeant authorises to say that you are fit and competent enough to go on independent patrol without a supervisor. So out you go like a baby chick without its mother for the first time.

Catching a carload of TWOCers (Taking Without the Owner's Consent, an epidemic crime in the 90s: joyriders, as they were often called) and ending up in the middle of a wooded area with absolutely no clue as to where we were. My crewmate and I caught four of the joyriders (after they rammed our car twice) but one had managed to escape. We ended up along a dark, uninhabited lane next to a disused farm building. It was pitch-black, and it took over an hour for our colleagues to find us. Our car was damaged beyond repair due to being rammed, and the only thing working were the lights and the blues strobe on top of the car roof.

The problem was exasperated because we had ended up in a neighbouring police force's area and our radio channel was tuned into their frequency. We had desperately tried to give our location, but they couldn't find us. We were eventually found by one of our inspectors (good bloke) who had worked out our confusing radio messages. I cannot begin to explain the truly joyous feeling I felt when I was standing on top of the roof of the police car and saw in the distance the blue flashing lights of the police vehicles as they came in our direction to rescue us. The cavalry had truly arrived. In those days, we had no phone, or satnav, only a police radio. We were the toast of the shift after that event because it was a particularly good arrest despite getting lost.

I remember going to a number of domestics and being told by the aggressor, "You can't come in, it's only a domestic." The aggressor was normally the male, but not always. We would then inform them that we are coming in under Section Blah Blah, breach of the peace etc.

A sad job was catching a well-known TWOCer one evening. I was on mobile patrol with another police officer in a Delta Alpha car (first response car) when we received a call on the radio from the control room informing us that a stolen car had been spotted near to our location. So we parked up, lights and engine off, and waited. After a short time we spotted the nicked car as it went into a housing estate directly opposite our location. We illuminated the Blues & Twos, and gave chase. As we got closer the car stopped and the driver and passenger decamped (got out of the stolen car and legged it). I went after the passenger and my crewmate went after the driver. I ran after my assailant who was about 20 yards in front of me. He then turned right and ran up a back alleyway which connected to a row of back gardens. I reached the entrance to the alleyway a few seconds later, but couldn't see my offender. On my right was a series of six-foot garden gates leading to their corresponding back gardens. I could see the first gate was swinging slightly ajar. I got out my Maglite torch, a useful truncheon in those days. I then saw a young lad hiding in the corner behind a dustbin. I shouted, "Get the fuck out of there!" in my sternest voice. He stood up, and I immediately recognised him as a very well-known TWOCer. I was sure it was the same person whom I had initially chased after, but I wasn't 100%. I arrested him and took him back to the police station. He knew the score and repeated, "No comment" throughout the interview. Criminals who knew the score invariably went 'no comment' and it's every person's right to do so, but it was very frustrating from the police officer's point of view. Well, this TWOCer's solicitor (brief) was a particularly nasty piece of work and got him released on a technicality.

If I had lied and said that I had seen him continuously, then that would have been enough to charge him. The fact was that I hadn't seen him continuously. I had morals and had to stick to them.

A year later, that TWOCer was killed together with another person in a stolen car trying to evade a pursuing police vehicle. The driver tried to negotiate a tight bend and drove off the road. Both young lads died and one other passenger suffered severe brain damage.

I could never understand how a defence solicitor could sleep at night knowing in his heart that he was helping a criminal get off, only for that individual to be released and potentially going out to commit the same offence all over again. If you do wrong and get away with it without being punished, then the chances are you'll go out and commit the same offence again, or worse.

It was around this time that I had another lucky escape. It was a Sunday and it was our nights week, and during the day I had been to the seaside with my wife up at Hunstanton, and we had travelled back home early evening to prepare for my night shift. During the journey home I noticed that my right arm had swollen up. I wasn't overly concerned because it didn't hurt.

When I reported for work at 10pm, I was crewed in a Delta Alpha car with my crewmate who was an ex-Army medic. As it was in the summer and we were all wearing short sleeves, he commented on my swollen arm and I said it was just a reaction to an insect bite that I must have picked up at the seaside. No problems. During the course of the shift, we had to go to the local hospital to deal with reports of a drunk causing problems in A&E. We arrived and quickly sorted it out. As we were completing a short PNB entry in the ward sister's office, she remarked on my arm. I said, it was just a reaction to an insect bite. "No, it's not," she said, "you've got a DVT, deep vein thrombosis, which in the arm is very rare." She then advised me to see a doctor straight away. So I told my crewmate (the ex-Army medic?) what the ward sister had said, and we sought out a doctor, who examined me immediately, then rushed me into Emergency. I was in hospital for about a week, attached to a drip and then I was on warfarin, an anticoagulant, to thin my blood.

During the course of my stay, I had a few doctors come to see me as they had never heard of a DVT in the arm before, only in the legs. They were at pains to explain how I got it. I was eventually discharged and remained on a form of anticoagulant for the next year and had regular check-ups with my local GP, who also had never heard of a DVT in the arm. Lucky for me, there were no side effects. And lucky for me, I attended the hospital when I did. My gratitude to that ward sister for spotting it.

A humorous incident one night occurred at a well-known infamous pub. The landlord had lost control of the pub, meaning it had been taken over by the hard boys, and there were a hardcore element of about a dozen men who had decided to help themselves to the drinks behind the bar. We knew there was a high possibility that this was going to turn into a bit of a punch-up.

The pub was situated at the end of an alleyway on quite a steep incline. We entered the pub mob-handed and confronted the hard boys. There were about six or so of them who were up for a scrap (alcohol, as we know, can fuel the aggressive nature in people) and the remainder of the punters were just bystanders, curious to see what was going to happen. After a quick cracking of heads, we nicked them all for public order and licencing offences. In most cases after the initial bravado, the adrenaline diminishes, and people become less aggressive (in most cases). We then escorted them out of the pub and walked them towards the police riot vans, which were parked at the end of a nearby alleyway. Now, to get to them, we had to negotiate a steep incline. You can imagine the scenario, two lines of men walking up the incline towards the riot vans. On one side were the offenders and on the other there were us, the police officers. Now the weather was bitterly cold (end of January-type weather) and as we walked up the alleyway, we all started to slip on the surface which had turned to ice. The offenders were helping the police and the police were helping the offenders, as we were all slipping on the icy surface. It was so comical and everyone started laughing. You know the infectious, 'I'm nearly wetting myself' laugh – well, like that. By the time we all got to the riot vans parked on the road, we were all in tears of laughter. 10 minutes earlier we all wanted to batter each other.

I encountered many, many incidents of a similar nature involving people who initially wanted to fight me. Then, after a brief or not so brief dialogue, they altered their aggressive stance. It really was a matter of my attitude and my behaviour affects your attitude and behaviour.

And of course, alcohol always played a part.

I remember an incident whilst in basic police training at Ashford. All the police recruits, about 140 of us, were involved in a mock scenario training-type exercise. This consisted of half of the recruits acting as police officers, and the other half acting as demonstrators. I was part of the later and it was meant to be a large public order disturbance involving a strike at a fictitious manufacturing factory. It ended in uproar as nobody acted by the script that they had been given, and it turned into a big, ugly fight. Police probationers acting as police officers versus police probationers acting as demonstrators.

My memory of the incident as a demonstrator was the fact that all of the police officers were wearing black gloves and for some unknown reason this was like a red rag to us demonstrators/police officers. It showed an aggressive stance by the police which provoked us demonstrators. Maybe they should have worn pink 'n' fluffy gloves instead.

In my first two years as a copper I had a two-week CID attachment, and a two-week traffic attachment. The CID attachment consisted of hardcore boozing for nearly the entire two weeks. At the time it was the early 90s, and it was still acceptable to use your Police Warrant Card, aka The Blue Rover, to gain access to all manner of establishments. Once inside, the alcohol and the entertainment were usually free. Being in CID increased the free entry options considerably.

However, there were memorable incidents when the CID earned their wages. The first incident that I was involved in was arresting and charging of two nasty pieces of work who went around the local area on a motorbike robbing from isolated forecourt petrol stations. Their modus operandi was to pull up and pretend to buy petrol, at the pumps. They would then produce the sawn-off shotgun, a particularly nasty piece and favoured by some villains, and threaten the frightened staff with it. All for a couple of hundred pounds and a few packs of cigarettes.

As it was a rather nasty crime, we had no problems in getting the necessary intelligence needed to arrest both offenders. I was involved in the initial interviews together with a seasoned CID detective. He managed to get a confession from both offenders by getting them to 'grass' on each other. Both blamed the other as being the actual shotgun carrier.

One of the offenders also informed us of the man who supplied the shotgun for the vicious robberies in the first place. It was typical 'old Sweeney-type policing', which sadly no longer exists anywhere anymore, except on the TV.

So you have to ask yourself: Do you bend the rules to get a criminal convicted of a crime? How far do you bend the rules and what line do you cross? What if the crime was up there as the worst of the worst? A serious assault and robbery on a vulnerable elderly person. Or a sickening sexual assault on a child or on an elderly person, and you knew who the offender was. It was an eye-opener, although I wasn't new to controversy, having spent time in N. Ireland; it still made me look at myself and question my ethics and morals.

Life isn't just black and white, there is a massive grey area and each individual's grey area differs from the next person's. I suppose compromise in life is so important.

During my two-week CID attachment there were a lot of visits to drinking establishments with the view to 'intelligence gathering'. One such visit to a famous establishment involved the *Sunday Sport* girls, two famous ex-cricketers, my CID colleagues and myself. We all ended up in the VIP lounge and, of course, free drinks all night.

This was the early 90s and 'Old Bill' could still get into places without paying an entrance fee and the drinks were provided free of charge for the duration of our visit. I had a memorable two-week attachment and still have friends now from all those years ago. One such ex-cop is one of my closest friends and we are still in touch and meet up on a regular basis. In fact he was best man at my wedding.

I recall my two-week traffic attachment as being a little less interesting. Driving around in fast, three-litre cars do nothing for me; however, there was one exception. My tutor officer and I attended a fatal RTA (road traffic accident involving a death) which involved two cars. The fatal occurred on a quiet country lane and the scene that confronted me was really appalling. One car (which had recently been stolen) was on the wrong side of the road when it had smashed head-on into the oncoming second car. When we arrived there were other traffic officers, dog handlers with their dogs, the fire brigade and ambulances already in attendance. There was no one in the stolen vehicle, only a lot of blood, mainly on the front passenger's side. The dog had had picked up a scent from this car, so dog and handler were tracking across an adjacent field. Trapped in the second car were the driver and the front-seat passenger. We were told by the half-conscious front-seat passenger that she and the driver were sisters. Both were in their mid-twenties and the driver was dead. The half-conscious sister was not aware of this initially. What made this scene truly awful was the fact that the fire brigade were trying to cut the conscious passenger out of her seat, while all the time the dead sister was in situ next to her in the driver's seat. It looked as though she had died from horrific head injuries because the car looked as though it had been hit by a tank. Of course we were all mindful of the possibility of an explosion due to carnage. Due to the amount of damage to the car, the fire crew couldn't risk trying to free the dead driver, thus causing further injury to the surviving sister, so the driver was left there. After the passenger was rescued by the firemen, she realised that her sister had died due to her injuries. In the meantime, the dog handler had tracked the scent to a haystack in the middle of a field nearby and discovered a seriously injured young teenage girl. It was thought that the driver had stolen the vehicle and had taken his girlfriend (the injured girl) for a joyride to show off his driving skills. He had been driving too fast on the wrong side of the road and smashed head-on into the car that the two sisters were in and which was on the correct side of the road. He had fled the scene almost immediately and carried his injured girlfriend across the field, leaving her next to the haystack, then he ran off, leaving her to fend for herself.

I realised that I didn't want to be a traffic cop: I wanted to go and catch the criminal with the dog handler. But I was reminded that our role was to determine the traffic impact factors and secure the evidence at the fatal RTA for future investigations.

I later heard that the driver of the stolen vehicle (he was never called the killer) was found by the dog handler. Let's hope the dog managed to have a chew or three. The killer later received a five-year prison sentence for his crimes (he'd be out with good behaviour in less than three). This occurred in the early 90s: I wonder what he's doing now.

After completing my two years' probation, I was accredited with a pass. Nothing spectacular, really. The sergeant just comes into the parade room and gives you a certificate saying, "Well done, you are now a police officer. Now, here's your shift pattern for the year." This consisted of:

Seven days early (6am-2pm).

Two days off

Five days lates (2pm-10pm)

Two days off

Seven nights (10pm-6am)

A quick swing (2pm-10pm) then...

Four days off.

So a 28-shift pattern. Then you would start all over again with a 6am start for the early shift.

It normally went something like this. On earlies you managed to get some paperwork done, then off we would go patrolling the streets of whatever area you were designated to.

Your call sign on the radio could be Delta Alpha 4/1, or Delta Alpha 4/2, and so on. Certain call signs denoted a mobile patrol, which was normally two officers, and other call signs denoted an officer on foot. Yes, we had police officers walking 'the beat' in those days. A police officer out on the streets gained valuable nuggets of information and at the same time gave the public some reassurance. In my time we used to put out four area police marked cars, the Delta Alphas, first response marked police vehicles. Then other officers on shift would carry out their own enquiries and catch up with their paperwork. Then around midday on earlies is when you might get your first shoplifter to deal with.

Another job for the early shift was to 'take over' the jobs left by the previous night shift. It wasn't uncommon for the early turn to arrive for duty and half the shift would be assigned to deal with prisoners in the police cells left over from the previous night's shenanigans. This was always a lottery, literally. You took over the paperwork from a night turn officer and if they were good then the handover went like a dream:

All statements done

All evidence bagged and accounted for

Scenes of Crime (SOCO) informed and all necessary paperwork completed

All you had to do was interview the prisoner: job done.

But if you had a handover that was a pile of poo.

Poor or non-existent statements available.

Evidence not booked in properly or unaccounted for.

SOCO not updated.

When this happened, you would have your work cut out for the remainder of the shift clearing up this particular pile of poo. It was a matter of pride with many officers. Hand over a file that you would like to receive. That mantra unfortunately was not observed by all.

There was a rumour – only a rumour, mind – going around that a bit of a cock-up on a handover had occurred sometime ago. Now every group dynamics has an alpha male, a top dog. Well, the police are no exception. There were a few alpha males in the police: some were sh*t hot, and some were just sh*t. Well, as the story goes, that one such sh*t alpha had nicked (arrested) a young lad for a very minor domestic. The lad had had an argument with his girlfriend one night and the neighbours had heard every verse and curse through the paper-thin walls and had called the Old Bill.

Now, alpha male rocks up in a squad car together with a young, pretty WPC (women police constable; they were WPCs in those days). Looking to impress the impressionable young WPC, alpha flexes his muscles and nicks the young lad on a breach of the peace/public order offence (the easiest way to nick anybody in those days).

So the young lad is searched and put into the back of the squad car and the officers check his wallet: you never know what might be concealed in one of the many small pouches. All perfectly legal when dealing with a person who has just been arrested. Among the usual paraphernalia in the wallet was a student ID card. Alpha decides to wind the lad up by calling him "Student Grant".

When they get to the police station custody suite (where prisoners are booked in and possessed), they found it to be very busy, with a number of prisoners waiting to be processed. So the custody sergeant, who is swamped, tells alpha to put his man into an interview room until they can catch up with the backlog of prisoners. So alpha tells Student Grant to take a seat, when all of a sudden a '10/10' shout is heard on the radio. 'Urgent assistance, now!!! If you hear a 10/10 shout on your radio it doesn't matter what you're doing, you go and assist whoever has called it in. Because one day it could be you facing a potential injury or life-threatening job, and you would like to hope that the cavalry were right behind you, or at least on its way. A 10/10 shout was a matter of pride with some officers, me included. I would only use it if it was really necessary, like it was me against overwhelming odds and I was about to get a good kicking or worse. Not the case with some, though: sometimes we would roll up and the offender would be handcuffed, but the officer had called the 10/10 shout because they had needed a handcuff key or a similar reason.

So back to the story. Alpha, eagerly wanting to impress the young WPC even more, is first out of the custody suite door to answer the 10/10 shout. As he's leaving, he calls out, "Student Grant's in interview room," to the harassed, dazed and overworked custody sergeant, and is out of the door.

Well, there's pandemonium in the streets and our young lad is left in the interview room, totally forgotten. Someone later recalls hearing something about a 'Stuart Grant', but there's no arrest report or any paperwork for a Stuart Grant. Meanwhile, alpha has got himself assaulted in the melee that ensued and had to go to A&E to get his broken nose seen to.

The early shift custody sergeant arrives and is faced with Armageddon in the custody suite. When a police officer finally gets to the interview room where our young lad is in and asks, "Are you Stuart Grant?" the lad truthfully replies that no, he isn't. He then gives his correct name, but no record can be found of the lad ever having been arrested. So as the story goes, the lad is released with a warning by the early shift custody sergeant, who has no idea as to who the lad is, what he is supposed to have done, or what he has been arrested for. When alpha comes back on duty some time later, and after his broken nose has been fixed, he ass who has dealt with that "little prick Student Grant". Of course, nobody had a clue as to who or what he is talking about.

Years later, that young impressionable WPC had become a seasoned police officer and related the story to me when I was crewed up with her on one night shift. She told me, "Not a lot of people know that."

If you were on the late shift (lates) 2pm-10pm, this was normally the busiest or the quietest, depending on the whim of the gods. It could be all nice and uneventful, when all of a sudden without any warning it would 'all kick off'.

I was on patrol in one of the Delta Alpha cars one afternoon and my crewmate actually said, "It's quiet at the moment." We literally turned around a corner to be confronted with an almighty punch-up in a field next to a pub. There must have been 20 fellows all going for it, no handbag stuff, a good, old-fashioned fist fight. We pulled up slowly, got out of the car, put our hats on (have you noticed that police officers rarely wear their hats now) when we heard the soft ripple of "the Old Bill, the Old Bill", and the fists gradually stopped flying. We went over to what was akin to the Alamo, and said those well-used words, "What's going on here, then?" A quick scan of those who had been involved and we could see there was only bruising and minor bleeding, a few ripped shirts here and there, and probably the odd loose tooth. We asked the landlord what had occurred. "Dunno," was the reply, ditto the staff and ditto everyone else in the pub. No one had seen anything, and no independent witnesses.

Now we could have nicked the lot of them for violent disorder (a mini-riot), tied up numerous police officers, and to what purpose? No complaints, no injuries, the custody sergeant would have had a pulmonary if we had arrested them all, and then taken the lot back to the nick. So we gave everyone a stern warning that any further conduct of this nature and we'd be back. "Sorry, Officer," was the unanimous reply from all involved. Phew!! Off we went like a shot. We didn't hear of any further disturbances from the pub. This reaction from the police to an incident of that nature would never occur today. Everyone would have been arrested, dozens of officers would have been tied up for hours, to what end?

It looks good on the stats. 20 people arrested for violent disorder and we would get 20 clear-ups, which looks good for the chief constable's weekly meetings. It would be in all of the local papers: "Local police deal robustly with blah blah blah". In reality, most of them would have been released without charge as there were no independent witnesses, and it would have tied up numerous officers for hours doing the necessary paperwork to satisfy the Crown Prosecution Service.

As a footnote, we'd never say, "It's quiet at the moment." We always use the 'Q' word. "It's Q at the moment." You didn't want to challenge the gods of Fate.

Sunday of lates was, without doubt, domestic city time. You could set your watch by it. The scenario:

The old man's been down the pub and comes back for his Sunday dinner a little merry. She's given him an earful over something, then off it would start. She goes for him or he goes for her.

As seasoned police officers we hated domestics because the cold, hard fact of the matter was that we couldn't really do much except nick one or both parties at the time and defuse the situation. Give each party a timeout and some breathing space. Normally, but not always, the man would get nicked. Sometimes he would put up a fight with officers, in which case she would then join in and have a go at us as well, so she'd also get nicked. Then he'd get all shirty 'cause we'd laid hands on his missus and then he would have another go. Occasionally we had a serious case of abuse and managed to get the injured party into a domestic shelter accommodation. But this was only a temporary measure and eventually the aggrieved party would return to the marital abode.

On a rare occasion the women would pack her bags and leave with the children. But the hard, cold fact was that, more often than not, he was the one who controlled the purse strings. This was in the 90s, don't forget. I'm sure the female doesn't put up with it as much nowadays, hopefully.

Other domestic incidents involved the aggressor saying, "It's only a domestic, you ain't coming in." "Really? Oh yes, we are," and in we'd go and find ourselves in the usual scenario where drink had played a major part in the argument.

I do not want to belittle domestic abuse, but in reality the abuse had started days, weeks, months or even years before we turned up. As I said, we hated dealing with domestics because we really had no idea of the reasons why they had occurred. We could just give both parties some breathing space and hope it didn't turn into anything more serious, which often was the case. When it all went 'pear-shaped', we, the police, the social services and such, would often get the blame. What about the people themselves taking responsibilities for their actions? Or the parents, their friends or relatives? Shouldn't they be held accountable, or is it just easier to blame the emergency services?

So that was lates. Usually unpredictable. Not so for the night shift.

Nights were our most productive time in dealing with the criminal elements of our society. After the shift had finished, if you hadn't made an arrest then your shift sergeant would want to know why, and you had better come up with a really good reason.

Each shift had a sector that they were responsible for and ours was the south sector, aka The Beautiful South. After all, burglars, car thieves, people stealing from cars, pub fights etc were our bread and butter, and the majority of the public wanted their police to deal with the offenders of these crimes. Very rarely did you go through the night shift without nicking someone, aka, getting a body. We would then hand it all over to the early shift, so when they came in on duty they would be confronted with the same pile of poo that they had probably left for us the previous week. It was all fun.

I was crewed in a Delta Alpha car one time on nights, and my crewmate's wife was expecting twins at any time. We got a call on the radio to go to an address and assist the CID (Criminal Investigation Detectives) with a serious assault. When we arrived at the address we found out that there had been a domestic and the male offender had beaten up his girlfriend. Both were alcoholics and the offender had been arrested for GBH, Grievous Bodily Harm, by the CID. (Both had been arrested on numerous occasions for domestics in the past and were well known to social services, the council and the housing department.)

The senior detective on the scene ordered my crewmate and me to escort the victim to the hospital while he and his detectives dealt with the offender and gathered evidence from the crime scene. The woman was taken on a stretcher to the ambulance which was parked nearby. I could see that she was unconscious and had appalling head injuries. I went with her in the ambulance while my crewmate drove the Delta Alpha car and followed us to the hospital.

They were expecting us as a crash crew team were on standby at the hospital waiting for our arrival. Because of the 'continuation of evidence' we both went with her when she was taken through to A&E so there would be no legal loopholes or technicalities at a later date. For example, a defence solicitor could accuse the police of 'cross-contamination' and get the offender acquitted, as often was, and still is, the case. Another reason for our continued presence with the victim was because we could record any words that she may have said when she regained consciousness. The paramedics passed the victim on to the medical staff, who in turn took her straight into surgery while my crewmate and I waited outside.

In those days we had no mobile phones. Communications (comms) was all done by a handheld radio – not a strong signal – or the car radio, which had a marginally stronger one. Now the hospital was a notorious black spot regarding comms, so we had no way of updating our control room as to the current situation. At the same time we couldn't hear anything back from them in the way of instructions. We finally received an update by using the telephone in the ward sister's office. My crewmate had stayed outside of theatre where the victim was and I went to the office to give them an update.

The control room operator was on the phone and almost frantic as she hadn't heard from us and wanted updates as to the situation. She was obviously under a great deal of pressure from her boss and from CID to get an update soonest. I said as soon as the victim was out of surgery, then I'd be in a better position to give updates. I was just about to hang up the phone when the controller told me to let my crewmate know that his wife had been taken into hospital, as her waters had broken. So I rushed back to my crewmate and told him about his wife. I could see the worry on his face. I told him to go to her, and to leave his PPE (personal protection equipment, baton, handcuffs etc) with me. I also told him not to worry, and that I'd handle any flak that may come our way.

(I knew some police officers who were so dedicated to the job that they would have stayed and not gone to see how their wives were. They lived for the job and were often the ones who had marital and drink problems. The job gets to some people in different ways.)

So off he went to find out how his wife was doing while I remained outside Theatre waiting for the updates. Sometime later, the surgeon came out and informed me that the victim had died on the operating table due to her injuries. For the record, he gave me the time of death and I noted this in my PNB. I would need this information to give to the control room and also some time in the future for the Coroner's Court. He also told me that an autopsy would be performed at a later date to determine the cause of death. Almost immediately my crewmate returned all jubilant. His wife had just given birth to a set of healthy twins, so he thought he'd better come down to see how I was doing and to update me on his good news. I informed him of what had happened with our victim and I think it dampened his joy for a moment as the births and the death occurred almost simultaneously. I asked him to wait for a moment while I went to update the control room before he went rushing back up to the maternity ward where mother and twins were all doing well.

I got through to my controller and told her, "It's now a murder." To cover our backs, I told her about my crewmate and his situation with his wife. "No problem," was the reply. So I made my way back to Theatre where my crewmate was waiting, eager to get back to the maternity ward. It was all in a day's work for a patrol police officer.

Another 'gimme' was the Friday night, Saturday nights are good for fighting. The New City had a number of nightclubs in the 90s, as I mentioned earlier. Cops got into most establishments but there were a few you wouldn't go in socially as a police officer. After all, society's criminal element had to have to a place to go for a drink like everyone else. So on a Friday night or a Saturday night or both (some officers liked it and volunteered) you were allocated to a Delta Tango outfit which meant the riot vans. You had the driver, the commander, usually a skipper (sergeant) and six blood-curdling coppers waiting in the back of the van to spill some blood. Preferably not their own.

I was getting on for 40 years of age and had had my fair share of punch-ups. However, once the old adrenaline kicked in you couldn't help but get the buzz even if you were getting on a bit like me.

One occasion stuck in my mind from all those years ago. There was an infamous drinking establishment that had a bad reputation for fights inside and outside of its premises. There was always trouble there and we would react accordingly. Now on one Saturday night one of our sergeants didn't have his waterproof jacket with him. So instead, he wore his old-style Dixon of Dock Green police overcoat together with his police helmet. Well, this attire went out with Ark.

So there he stood together with the bouncers (doormen), and said, "Good evening" to all the punters as they arrived at the venue. Now, some hours later, when it was 'kicking-out time', which incidentally coincided with 'kicking-off time', as the punters left, they all recalled seeing the old-fashioned copper on the door when they first arrived and he was there when they departed. No trouble whatsoever. He was almost a calming influence on the punters.

Well, that set a trend, because the next set of nights about four of us did exactly the same. We stood outside the clubs in our Dixon of Dock Green overcoats and helmets and greeted everybody. The bouncers thought it was a gimmick or a wind-up, but it seemed to work. There was very little trouble because nobody fancied having a ruck with Dixon of Dock Green. I think we dressed up again the following month in the same attire and the response was the same: "Evening, all" and no trouble.

In the early 90s, there was a major rave club on the outskirts of the new city of Milton Keynes.

It was in a warehouse-type venue, and attracted ravers from miles around. It was vast, with hundreds of whistle-blowing, funny-dancing people, going on until the early hours, and very little alcohol was consumed, only water, which was good news for the police. The flip side of this was the fact that there was a major drug epidemic associated with the venue. Speed, uppers, downers, poppers etc. Some of these ravers came from well-to-do families, and words were whispered in certain ears as to why all these children of rich and influential people were coming in at 7ame stoned out of their tiny minds. So an operation (op) was formulated. Probably the best op that I had ever been involved with in the police. Undercover officers staked out the place for weeks prior, after which we got the green light to go in. The plan was very simple.

There would be three independent groups of officers involved in the op.

1) The undercover officers (self-explanatory).
2) The PSU units (heavy mob/arrest teams), each team consisting of 7x u4I (up for it) officers, and lastly...
3) The test purchases (TPs). Now, TPs were a rare breed of coppers. They were chosen for their role as a TP because their looks, normally very demure, young-looking and not at all like the usual everyday police officer. They were used on surveillance jobs where they wouldn't be noticed or draw attention to themselves, and for buying drugs from dealers.

So the plan. The TPs would be in the venue with marked £5 and £10 notes together with the undercover officers, all pretending to be ravers. At an opportune moment the TPs would buy drugs from a dealer and go into the toilets to confirm the 'score' was authentic. Once confirmed, they would seek out the undercover officer with a prearranged signal indicating that they'd just 'scored'.

The undercover officer then strolled out of the venue all nonchalantly, and had a quick fag and a chat with somebody just like numerous other ravers. They then gave the prearranged signal to the skipper in a nearby riot van. The skipper then said, "Right, lads, we're on." We all got out of the riot van and adopted the normal police riot position when moving through a crowd. We all had high-viz jackets on: we didn't want to get lost in there, and held onto the utility belt of the police officer in front of you in an underhand grip. The officer behind you then took hold of your utility belt, and so on. You get the gist.

So off we went, the skipper in front, closely followed by the rest of us. We then headed for the undercover officer, who had clandestinely ambled back into the venue. Just imagine, there were hundreds of people milling around outside, so there was very little chance of the ravers or the bouncers connecting us with the undercover officer. We went past the surprised-looking bouncers and into the venue. The undercover officer would then lead us to where the TP was.

At this point, we had no idea who the TPs were. Imagine us walking one behind the other, with the skipper following the undercover officer, who had re-established contact with their TP.

Imagine this venue with ear-shattering rave music, and hundreds of ravers with whistles, all madly dancing to the most outrageously loud rave music.

The TP would then lead us to where the dealer was, identify the drug dealer by some sign to the undercover officer who would then signal to our skipper. Then we would pounce. All hell broke loose. We then dragged the dealer out, passed by surprised-looking ravers, out of the door, and past even more surprised-looking bouncers, and into the nearby riot van. Then back to the police station with the stunned drug dealer. He would be booked in, the marked cash would be found on him and he would be processed. We then loaded up and went back to the venue for further instalments.

As we were booking our dealer into custody, a second PSU had successfully arrested a second drug dealer using the same technique.

We repeated this a further seven times, and the last one was the most mind-blowing of all. We repeated the technique as previously carried out, but this time we ended up grabbing three men: one was the TP and the other two were drug dealers. We never knew who was who, because whichever one was the TP, they stayed silent throughout the journey in the back of the riot van. He just played the part as an innocent raver who had been accidentally caught up in the net. Back at the police station all three were booked in by the custody sergeant who carried on with the charade to preserve the TP's cover. Obviously the TP was released eventually, but we never knew which one it was. One of the few successful ops that I was involved with in the police.

CHAPTER 8

I was involved in a complicated fraud during my time on shift. I had arrested a very clever individual who was conning a well-known high street store out of hundreds of pounds. At the time, this particular store allowed a customer to buy goods up to the value of £500 using a cheque without the need to produce a cheque guarantee card. Amazing.

So this individual would go into the store and buy anything, and I mean anything, up to that value by using just a cheque and without any other form of a cheque guarantee card. He would then walk out of the store for a few minutes then go back into the same store. He would say he wanted a refund for the goods that he had just purchased, and ask for a cash refund for the entire amount. His scam was that he acquired five bank chequebooks, that's 25 cheques in each book, but he had no money in his account. After about ten days the bank started to get two or three cheques per day to the value of around £500, which obviously all bounced.

I spent weeks on that job trying to gather the evidence against a very cunning person. I always had a slight admiration for criminals who used their brain to commit fraud, as opposed to those who used a shotgun or violence to scare someone senseless for a few lousy pounds. Also, in those days I was given the time to investigate a crime of this complexity. Nowadays, it wouldn't happen, and the store would either investigate the crime themselves or just write off the loss and pass it on to the consumer.

Christmas time on shift was always a lottery. In effect, you normally had Christmas Day or New Year's Day off. As an unwritten rule, though, if you had a family in those days, the job would try and give you some time at home, if you were unfortunate enough to have to work on Christmas Day. It was around 1995, and I was on a shift on Christmas Day, when we got a call that there was a mass brawl on one of the estates. We were running a skeleton crew because even the villains normally took Christmas Day off (normally, but not always). As my crewmate and I arrived at the location of the incident, we were confronted with a mass fight outside a house. After wading in and trying to separate the main protagonists, it emerged that it was a family argument revolving around the Christmas dinner table as they all sat down to Christmas dinner. It ended up with all offenders being arrested and charged with affray, which is slightly less serious than violent disorder. I recall the main offenders were the father and his three grown-up sons. The next day, all four visited the police station. But instead of being taken there under arrest, like the previous day, they all attended voluntarily and with great shame. All were apologetic, saying that their conduct was appalling and they praised the way they had been treated, even though they were acting as louts the previous day.

I had a lucky escape in early 96. I was on an early shift and crewed up with an old warhorse who had been a uniformed police officer for about 25 years and all on shift – that's a long time. We were on mobile patrol, Delta Alpha in the city centre, when we got an 'immediate' shout (radio message), saying a violent domestic was taking place. So my crewmate, who was driving, hit the Blues & Twos (roof lights) and activated the siren. Off we went like Batman and Robin in the Batmobile.

Now, when you get an immediate shout, you are authorised to break all speed limits and go through any red lights that you encounter. The proviso was that you had to be careful. Well, Batman went racing through two red lights at warp factor 10 (am I getting two films mixed up here?) without getting us killed. Then as we approached the third red light, I could see a car coming at speed on our left, my side. I shouted, "Watch it, he's not seen us!" – next moment, **CRASH!!** The car smashed into us, broadside. The air bags didn't work and our car spun round 180 degrees, with us being thrown around like we were on a fairground ride. We eventually walked out of the car alive, and with both legs and arms in good order. I then saw the driver of the other car, who was a lady, and she also got out without a scratch.

Both cars were a total write-off. We had to call it in to the control and a traffic supervisor arrived quickly on the scene. Whenever an RTA (road traffic accident) involved a police vehicle, then a supervisor had to be called. An ambulance arrived at the same time as the supervisor and surprisingly no one was even slightly hurt. Looking at our seriously damaged car, he was astonished that we got out alive.

I often got an "Are you PC Brewer? You arrested my brother, son etc, but he's turned out OK, best thing that ever happened to him." These comments, and those of a similar vein were the best forms of feedback that I could ever wish for. The commendations that were awarded by the chiefs at force headquarters, with a ceremony to boot, were for the most part quite meaningless. Maybe it's just me being sore because I never got a commendation? No! Feedback on the streets by offenders or those associated with offenders was the best yardstick to measure your competence in dealing with society's underclass.

A rather comical job involved a report of a pot-bellied pig being in the caller's back garden. It was a Sunday afternoon late shift, 2pm-10pm, and my crewmate and myself attended the address and got a glimpse of the offending pig. We ended up chasing this little bleeder for over a mile up and down the canal, until we managed to grab it and tie it up. During the operation, the control room received a call from the owner so we were able to reunite both animal and owner. Job well done.

One night we were in a Delta Alpha car when we got a call from the control room asking us to go and assist two CID officers. We were only minutes from the address in question and when we arrived we could see the two officers having a bit of a struggle with the man of the house outside his front door. So we strolled up to the house and asked if there was anything we could do, said with a bit of a smirk. "Just f**king hold him, so I can cuff him," was the frustrated reply. So my crewmate and I waded in and took hold of the suspect, who was still struggling. Then the CID officer put the handcuffs on my crewmate. With arms all over the place, she had cuffed the wrong person. To add insult to her embarrassment, she didn't have any cuff keys with her. We eventually sorted it out, though. I later heard that she received a Christmas present in the shape of a handcuff key for years to come.

March 1994 to June 1996 was the most productive time in my police career. My probation had finished and I really believed I was making a difference. I managed to fit in a stint of nine months as an area beat officer (ABO) together with very good copper. At the time we were responsible for one of the worst estates in Milton Keynes. When I say 'worst', it had a bad reputation, but as I discovered, most of the people were good citizens who just wanted a simple life. A few wayward families gave an inaccurate impression of the problems encountered on the estate. As I had experienced in my childhood it was easy to get a reputation that was unwarranted and inaccurate.

In those days virtually every estate had its own ABO and he/she was responsible for knowing exactly what was going on on their estate. It was a matter of pride and on more than one occasion an ABO was asked about a particular 'target' and provided in-depth intel (intelligence) on a certain individual. Sometimes an ABO lived on the estate that they policed and everyone new him/her.

As an ABO at the time, I managed to get a moped licence and there were a pool of half a dozen 90cc mopeds at the station, exclusively for the use of the ABOs. Woe betide anybody taking one of these instruments of wrath if they were not authorised to do so.

As Milton Keynes is a warren of redways (Google it), it made sense for the community bobbies to have this mode of transport. 'Bollococks'. We used to race around the redways at night, looking for the joyriders. We also had pushbikes as well, but bagging a moped was always preferable. A strange thing with the mopeds was the fact that you could put your briefcase on the footrest between your feet and the centrifugal force kicked in and the briefcase stayed in place as you bombed around the estates. We all had briefcases in those days. They came in handy as a shield, and as they were full of paperwork and quite heavy, it was also a useful tool to hit people with.

One afternoon, myself and another ABO responded to a radio call from the control room:

"Joe Bloggs etc, at such an address, reports of a knife, and threatening other residents." We responded and turned up at said address in a matter of minutes. Briefcase in one hand, truncheons in the other, we went to the address of the alleged knife-wielding maniac, hoping that the briefcases would protect us from a knife attack. He did have a kitchen knife; however, we knew him quite well as he was one of those 'care in the community' cases. It means he's not quite mad enough to be sectioned under the Mental Health Act, therefore deemed fit and not a menace to the public.

There were a number of these poor unfortunates living in little communal flats and most of the time there was a carer available, but not always. Also, these people were free to do what they pleased and to go where they pleased. Most of the time they were harmless, gentle individuals. But on occasions we did have the odd problem, especially if they hadn't taken their medication.

So as we approached his flat he came out with the knife. We told him in no uncertain terms to put the knife down, otherwise we were going to batter the bejeebers out of him. He of course complied. We did a quick PNB entry and advised him regarding his conduct. We stayed with him for a little while and just listened to him and tried to contact his carer. We reassured all the other residents in the block, then off we went. The problem with this gentleman and others like him was that if we arrested him, which we had done in the past, the custody sergeant back at the police station would have released him almost immediately, because he was unfit to be detained. In other words, he wasn't the full ticket, and we would have probably been given a bollocking by the custody sergeant for wasting his time, as we 'should've known the score'. (In those days the custody sergeant was like a god, having the power to release or to detain any individual who came into their custody suite.)

So then we would take our knife-wielding 'care in the community' person to the secure mental unit at the hospital, under Section 136 of the Mental Health Act. This was a 'power' to detain people who were considered to be a danger to themselves and to others. With this Act, you didn't necessarily have to commit a crime, just be a little not quite the full ticket. I had obviously used this power on numerous occasions in the past because it's still vivid in my memory to this day. So off we take matey boy to the secure unit to be assessed as to his mental state.

The first time I went to the secure unit, I went into the office being the new boy. There were three men and one woman there and at the time I was not sure who were the staff and who were the residents. Because matey boy was not quite mad enough to be detained further, he passed their tests as to his mental capacity, and therefore he was released from the secure unit.

So it was a vicious circle. He wasn't compos mentis, rational enough to be detained in a police station and wasn't mental enough to be detained in a secure mental unit.

After experiencing the runaround for the umpteenth time when confronted with a matey boy incident, we just did the best that we could.

As an ABO in the 90s, we were generally left alone to police our estate. Sunday mornings were normally warrants time, if you had the time of course. We would go to the warrants office at the station and look through outstanding warrants for people on our estate. There were many types of warrants:

A) Outstanding fines

B) Bail warrants, where they hadn't answered their bail

C) Non-payment of TV licence (honest): on the poorer estates we tended to ignore these

D) Non-committal

E) Committal or a summons warrant were best of all because we could arrest them and bring them before the courts. If it was a Sunday, he'd be in the cell overnight and face the judge the following morning. If the offender was a particularly nasty piece

ONE HEAD MANY HATS

of work, he would be nicked on a Saturday afternoon, after the courts had closed for the week. Which meant he was in the cells on Saturday afternoon (no football), all day Sunday, and then he would be before the judge on the Monday morning. But that ploy was only used for the really nasty deviants in our society.

I served a warrant on this family man one Sunday morning. It was a bail warrant, which meant he hadn't answered his bail. (When you're arrested for a crime and there is insufficient evidence to charge you at the time, but officers think they may need more time to gather more evidence, then you'd be bailed to return in, say, two weeks' time to answer any further questions. Part or this agreement was that the suspect agreed to return on the date stated. If they didn't they were informed that they would be arrested and taken to the police station. He may then be interviewed regarding the crime or he could be re-bailed for whatever outstanding offence he had initially been arrested for in the first place – nothing major.)

Well, on this particular occasion I was on foot and on my own when I knocked on his door. The plan was to arrest him then call up a Delta Alpha car to come and escort us both back to the police station. "No mobiles available to assist PC Brewer," came the call from the control room. So I explained to the prisoner (he was my prisoner now because I had arrested him) that we would walk back to the station together, about a mile away. No dramas. I told him what was going to happen, that he and I were just going for a stroll. No need for handcuffs. So off the two of us went on a pleasant Sunday morning stroll to the nick. A few curious glances from the odd dog walker, but nobody really looked too closely and we were not bothered at all. Once at the nick, he was quickly processed, re-bailed and out of the station all within an hour. I think I even managed to grab a car and take him home. He thanked me later.

The point of this short parable is that this would never happen today. I was able to police in this manner because I had already established a rapport with the residents on the estate and they all knew me. This was achieved by endless hours spent in the local schools, going to parish meetings, walking the streets and talking to people, helping out at the local youth club, people knew who their local police officers were. Ask a hundred people today, and they will have no idea who their local officer is. As there are hardly any police officers walking the beat now, the public do not get to engage with the 'boys and girls in blue'. Because I had established a rapport (as had my predecessors) with people on my estate, I was able to take this man into custody the way that I did.

I tried to never make it too personal, as I wasn't aware of people's circumstance. It wasn't for me to judge. Saying that, though, I am a human being, and did take some crimes personally. On these occasions I did all I could to get the offender banged up.

Warrants were a useful tool in a lot of ways. Summons warrants, as I said, meant arresting and bringing the offender before the courts. Now if you saw the recipient of such warrant, it had to be served on them and they would then be arrested. However, it was doing them a favour if you knocked on their door, especially during evening dinner time. It would normally be the wife who answered the door (men hardly ever answered the front door when their dinner was on the table). So we would tell the missus that we had a warrant to serve on the old man. You could set the second hand on your watch by the sounds of someone legging it out of the back door. We, the Old Bill, and the wife of the offender, would lock eyes and we would say something like, "He needs to get this sorted," or words to that effect. Then we would tell her that her husband/partner could go to the courts in the morning and it would be dealt with there and then. But if we have to come back, then we will arrest him in front of the children and he'll spend a night in the cells.

She's thinking about this. More often than not, he would turn up the next day at the courts because he didn't want to put his family through the grief. Or his missus probably gave him an earful and told him to go and get it sorted out, or he'd be sleeping on the couch until he did. As a footnote, if we intended to serve the summons on someone, then we would always have one officer around the back waiting for our man to run out of the back door. I think we were crafty but fair.

As ABOs, it was a matter of pride that you knew all the bad men on your estate. There were different levels of 'bad', from very minor to very serious villains. We had to have some bottle as ABOs because we would knock on their door, introduce ourselves and ask to come in. We were always allowed into the person's home. Sometimes they had their wife or children in the house, and we would have a 'quiet word'. We would tell them that we knew who they were and that we dealt with the problems on the estate: any problems you come to us. Thanks for the tea, and that normally did the trick, especially when we were involved with the youth clubs or the local boxing clubs. This was because the kids knew who we were and passed this on to their parents. So when the time came to have to nick Dad, he was less likely to 'kick off' if his children were there. He was even less likely to have a go because his kids probably liked us, the area beat officers.

CHAPTER 9

Shortly after my police probation finished, I joined the Royal Military Police Territorial Army (RMPTA). I completed my basic training and joined 164 Provo Company, and served as a Red Cap for five years. (So I was in the RMPTA as well as a regular police officer with Thames Valley Police.) The thing about my basic training was that I was 40 years old and the average age of the rest of the recruits were in their mid-twenties. It was an interesting and challenging two weeks' training, and I bonded with the young Scottish and Welsh soldiers who were also on the course with me.

I was very proud when I was awarded my Red Beret from the instructors after successfully completing my basic training.

So I spent the next five years attending 164 RMPTA's two-week training exercise which was held once a year. I have to admit that we did more drinking than actual policing, but it was fun and they paid us handsomely. I also managed to get a motorbike licence through the RMPTA, having an intensive five-day motorbike riding course. The triple beauty of this particular experience was the fact that:

1) I got paid by the RMPTA to train to ride a bike.
2) Thames Valley Police paid me because I got leave to attend the five-day course.
3) I got the best training from an Army motorbike instructor, a

motorbike licence, and it didn't cost me a penny, and the bike that I learnt to ride on was a 350cc Harley.

My second daughter entered the world around this time of my life. She was also born in Milton Keynes Hospital. No such dramas as daughter number 1's birth.

So after four years with a mixture of on the beat policing and running the area car, I applied for the Protection Group (Prot Gp). This was a firearms department which consisted of about 100 officers all armed with H&K (Heckler & Koch MP5) semi-automatic machine guns and a 9mm Glock 17 Parabellum pistol. The MP5 is one of the most widely used sub-machine guns in the world and was popular with numerous military, police and intelligence services. The department was responsible for providing armed protection for 'principals' when they were in residence and ensuring the locations remained secure during the principals' absence. I was posted to the Royal Lodge in Windsor in the mid-90s and some famous and not so famous principals in no particular order were:

The Queen Mum, at her residence at the Royal Lodge at Windsor Great Park.

Prince Andrew when he was in residence at Sunninghill Park, just off Windsor Great Park and not far from the Royal Lodge.

Princes William and Harry when they went to Eton College in the late 90s.

John Major in his last year as PM, at his weekend retreat at Chequers.

Tony Blair in 97, when he and his family were at Chequers.

King Hussein of Jordan, when he was at his home just off Windsor Great Park.

Prince Bandar, who was the Saudi Ambassador to the USA at the time and had a massive house and estate just outside in a village just outside of Oxford. He was protected by Prot Gp officers, his private Saudi security, a number of ex-members of the SAS, and a private security detail made up of local men patrolling the grounds in Land Rovers. The joke at the time was that if it ever kicked off, i.e. the estate was being attacked, then we would give our guns over to the ex-SAS guys as they would be more proficient than us coppers. In the 90s Prince Bandar was described as the 7th-richest man in the world.

In between carrying out my Royal and Dip duties, I also patrolled in the ASV (Armed Response Vehicle). There was a small group of officers who manned the ASV full-time and a few who manned it on an ad hoc basis, and I was one of the latter. The vehicle was the latest 2.4 litre Vauxhall Cavalier and was an armoury on wheels. It carried an assortment of weapons together with two armed police officers ready to respond to an armed or dangerous incident. The ASV was on the road 24/7 and we did a 12-hour shift, then another two officers would relieve us. It covered an area south of Oxford to the Bucks border with London, and as far west as Newbury. A vast area.

The job of a Prot Gp officer sounded quite exciting. In reality it was boring and tedious, guarding these people day and night, but the pay was good. My main recollections were the total cock-ups or misbehaving to while away the boredom and tedium. The main highlights of my tenure were:

Taking my late mum and my two young daughters to meet The Queen and the rest of the Royals at the private church situated in the grounds of the Royal Lodge, the residence of The Queen Mother. Also taking my mum to the Christmas carol service held once a year at Eton College and meeting Prince William. She loved that.

Prince William was also in the Army Cadets whilst at Eton, and in his last year he went to the Army Training Camp in Kent. He was accompanied by his personnel protection officer (PPO/bodyguard) and because I was ex-military, I got to go as well. It was a right old jolly, spending a week at an army camp and helped in training the future King of our country. I always take a personal pride when I see Prince William. Sad, I know, but true.

I met Tony Blair for the first time in early May 1977. He had just won his first term as Prime Minister and he and his family went to the PM's country retreat at Chequers just outside Aylesbury. Chelsea were in the FA Cup final that year, and he and his children had been invited to watch the match at Wembley. How did they manage to get ten FA Cup final tickets at such short notice?

I recall being on armed protection duty that day and the PM had arranged for two five-a-side football goals to be erected on the front lawn, and he and his children, plus the staff, had a pre-FA Cup final football match. A few of the armed officers joined in, too, and there is a picture of the event floating around somewhere. It was a wonderful occasion: he was such a charismatic character and all of the armed officers thought he was a truly honourable man. (Enough said about that mistake.)

My final fond memory was getting a lift in The Queen Mum's car, a limousine. She wasn't in the car at the time, as the driver had dropped her off at the main house. At the time, I had been on foot patrol in the grounds near to the house, and was walking back to the police control room, which was situated next to the main front gate, about half a mile away from the main house. As I was walking along the side of the road, I heard a car pull up just behind me. The driver wound down the window and asked if I wanted a lift. So I got into the back seat (I'm sure it was still warm from the previous occupant) and got a lift in the Royal limo. I did a few regal waves en route – alas, no one was present to see me. As the car pulled up at the main gate to exit the park, I saw a police officer, who was on duty at the time, rush out and was just about to give me a royal salute. I had a quiet chuckle as I alighted from Royal limo. He called me a few expletives when he realised it was only me.

I was on duty in the Police Post at the Royal Lodge when we heard the sad news that Princess Diana had died. It was early morning and we got a call on the 'hotline' informing us that there had been an incident and had we heard anything? We were asked if there were any press at the main gate, or anyone acting out of character.

The initial news was that Dodi had died, but there was no news regarding Princess Di. There were three of us on duty at the time and we all guessed that she had died. We were sworn to secrecy and not to say anything to anyone. The news was made public some hours later by the media. Over the next week or so there were hundreds of people flocking to the main gates of the Royal Lodge and placing bunches of flowers at the entrance gates. Strange really, because as far as we knew, Princess Di had hardly ever visited the Royal Lodge during her lifetime.

Another element to the job of a protection group officer was being a member of the police search team. We received quite extensive training and one of our major operations was to search the Royal Ascot horse racing event which is held in June each year. All the Royals and numerous VIPs attend this event, and therefore the ground is searched extensively. This mammoth task was bestowed on the men and women of the Protection Group. Once this task had been completed, I would change out of my search gear and into my best police tunic, draw my Glock pistol out of the armoury, and then stand outside the Royal enclosure. There was always a team of six armoured police officers and we would rotate between ourselves, ensuring The Queen and the Royal family received the best protection possible. This lasted for four days and it was quite an honour to be on duty when The Queen and The Queen Mother (they always arrived together) drew up in their horse and carriage and entered the Royal enclosure. I wonder if she remembered me from the Royal Albert Hall in 1972, lol.

Because we were all searched trained, some of us were also part of the Mobile and Operational Support (MOPS) Body Recovery Unit. Quite a mouthful. In essence, if there was a major incident within the Thames Valley area, then the MOPS team would attend and assist where necessary. Being trained in the body recovery aspect is self-explanatory. I served five years on the Protection Group and made a lot of friends during my time on the department, and have numerous memorable moments.

I returned to Milton Keynes police station in 2002 and took up the role as the ABO on the same notorious estate that I'd spent time on in the mid-90s. A full circle, you might say. Policing had changed out of all proportion from my time in the mid-90s. Being on Prot Gp, I had no idea of the changes that had occurred during my five years hobnobbing with Royalty and VIPs. In my opinion we were no longer a police force but a service with policing as an element, a sideline, so to speak. I have bumped into many serving officers over the years and virtually every one says the same thing. Basically it's rubbish; maybe others would say it's progress. However, wherever progress occurs, complacency, incompetence and corruption often ensue.

In 2018, I met a serving police officer whom I had served with many years previously. She was still a sergeant and told me that the latest initiative was called "The Hub". This consisted of the majority of police officers sitting at a desk and carrying out enquiries on the phone. She went on to tell me how disgusted she was and that on her previous shift, she counted 19 police cars in the police station. The point was that that those 19 cars should have police officers in them and both car and police officer should be out on patrol and not sitting behind a desk. Again, have you noticed that there are absolutely no police officers on patrol anymore?

I spent a few months as the local beat officer, then a short period on a couple of bizarre departments, then I ended up on the Area Intelligence Team (AIT). One of the AIT officers was one that I had previously served with, so we knew each other quite well. He helped me tremendously in the early days and he is one of my closest friends to this day. Another officer helped me by showing me the ropes, and ended up as my best man at my wedding many years later.

The AIT office was quite large and contained intelligence officers who were responsible for robbery, car crime, sex offenders, out of force crime, prostitution and all manner of specialist crimes. Most of the officers had their own remit, and intelligence was sacrosanct. Virtually all the AIT staff were ex-CID officers, me being the exception, as I was ex-firearms.

In many ways there was an undercurrent of 'them and us' when it came to CID and Uniform. However, I never experienced any alienation from the ex-CID boys. In fact they seemed to bend over backwards to help me, which made me even more suspicious. Greeks and Gifts and all that.

I started my AIT life compiling drug packages for the drugs team. I had the utmost respect for the men and women on the Drugs Squad. They were, as a rule, the best officers, and had to deal with some serious criminals. We also worked closely with the informant handlers, who often gave us a heads-up on some intel before it went onto the system.

So this is how the procedure worked with the Intelligence teams. First of all a police officer called the 'Reader' would get the information (Info), and grade it depending on its validity. He would put it onto the system and this info would then become intelligence (intel).

The difference between info and intel was this. Info was information that you looked at, but you couldn't act on that info on its own. For instance, Mrs Miggins saying Fred Bloggs is doing XYZ was info. But if you then had Mrs Brown also saying that Fred is doing XYZ, then that would then become intel, in which case we could act on it, i.e. obtain a warrant from a magistrate.

It was always about being reasonable and proportionate in the circumstances. It just meant that the initial info had to have some form of independent collaboration to safeguard the individual's rights.

Of course in the real world 'dealers' would inform on a rival if it gave them an advantage and kudos. Sometimes the informant handlers got information, but wouldn't let it go any further as it may have compromised one of their informants.

On occasions, intel was received on a certain individual and it could involve car crime, burglary and drugs, as they were all interlinked. So it would be counterproductive if say Car Squad were running an op on one of their hot targets while the Drugs Squad were also preparing to create a job on the same target. Even though it was monitored, there were occasions when more than one department were planning an operation on the same individual. Usually it came down to which department boss had the most clout or which one was the most persuasive. On occasions it just depended on which operation gave Thames Valley Police the most kudos with the press.

A drugs package consisted of looking at low-level drug dealers, checking the intelligence we had on them, compiling the paperwork, and then getting a warrant from a local magistrate to search a suspected drug dealer's premises. It was all a game. Everyone knew who was dealing and half the time the dealers were all informing on each other.

Most of them were from the low end of the social scale and had no compulsion in drug dealing from their homes where young children played. Surprisingly, a large percentage of low-level dealers were women. They tended to deal to friends and family and were, on the most part, not a great deal of a problem.

One infamous female dealer would keep a small flask containing a 'Class A' drug concealed in her vagina. Every time a punter came to her home she would go to the toilet, remove the flask, take out the necessary amount, then pass this on to her accomplice, who would then sell the 'Class A' to the punter. The reason why she was so successful was because we, the police, couldn't carry out an internal search of a woman's intimate area, but a doctor could. But the doctor wouldn't carry out any form of internal examination without the consent of the dealer, who of course wouldn't give said consent. Drugs intelligence defied all normal ethics of social life. We dealt with people who lived in a separate world from the rest of society with their own rules and absolutely no ethics or any form of moral code. It was a case of survive for the moment, fuck the past and fuck the future.

AIT summed it up for me when I was pressurised to carry out a 'big drugs operation' on a well-known infamous estate. Now I knew the estate well and I was always kept abreast of the situation by the local beat sergeant. This particular officer had been acting sergeant for a few years, but hadn't managed to pass the Sergeant exam for one reason or another. But he was an excellent copper and an excellent manager.

I had regular meetings with this sergeant, as I did with all the other sergeants in charge of the estates. He gave me honest and accurate appraisals of who was doing what. Car crime and burglary led to an increase in drug crime and vice versa. It all went hand in hand.

There was no significant increase in any of these three core crimes, so it was a surprise that the powers that be insisted I ran a major robbery and drugs operation on this estate. As this was over 15 years ago, I don't think I am committing any conflict of interest.

This operation (op) had a name, all ops had a name, and there was a computer-generated system that ploughed out these op names. This was because there were all manner of ops going on, and it wasn't beyond the realms of possibility that two ops running parallel could have the same op name. So to prevent this happening, every op that was conceived had its own unique name taken from the computer-generated list. My op was some obscure name, like Op Kallionrotudas (Op K). Whenever we got the op name we would have to refer to the dictionary to find out what the flipping name actually meant.

Now this Op was so secretive that the meetings were not held at the station but at a clandestine location a few miles away. Also, all of the intel pertaining to the Op was locked away so no one could see it. The operation itself consisted of four two-man teams of firearm officers, that's eight heavily armed officers. We also had a team of 'Urbans': these were highly skilled police officers who literally dug a hole in a ground and stayed in one location for days at a time, just observing.

Then we had the Test Purchases (TPs) and this time they were made up to look like vulnerable schoolchildren. Strangely, the local sergeant was not at the meeting.

So day one, and the hall where the briefings were being held was full of all manner of individuals ready to put this plan into operation. The problem was that, although the plan was a good one, there was no substance to it. It sounded plausible, but in reality there would be no major success because there was no major problem. A bit like the SAS Iranian hostage siege team being used against the pupils of *Please Sir!* or *Grange Hill* (depending on your age).

After four days of running Op K, we caught a few petty criminals and low-level drug dealers, and that was all. Now the police press officer made out that the Op was a major success in dealing with a major robbery and drug criminal outfit. He made it sound as though we had captured the Great Train Robbers. Talk about inflating the importance of the intelligence, a little like the WOMD in Iraq.

When the local sergeant found out what was going on on his patch without his knowledge, he was furious with me. As I was sworn to the 'need-to-know basis' and he wasn't on the list, I could only apologise to him. I didn't think he would ever forgive me, and our 'special relationship' was in serious jeopardy. I felt like King Solomon.

Some time later, a lowly intelligence researcher (I won't say her name but if she ever reads this she'll know it's her) did a brilliant job of discovering a crime trend on that particular estate.

At the time, all the AIT officers had analysts and researchers working with them. As the name suggests, they did all the donkey work and found trends and patterns to a particular crime, thus predicting 'hot spots' and enabling the hierarchy to place their resources for the best possible results of a success. Surprisingly, they were sometimes quite accurate, but on other times they were so off the mark that they were on a different planet, like in the case of Op K.

Now this lowly researcher did a bit of clever analytical work and found a gem of intel. I didn't pass this on through the proper channels, i.e. the handlers or the reader, but passed this directly to the local area sergeant, who had been annoyed with me regarding Op K.

He and his merry bunch of men and women bashed in a few doors and found a massive load of drugs, money and firearms. No major Op, no briefings or meetings, just good, old-fashioned policing.

I think I was vindicated by the area sergeant after that. Many times later I would be privy to an operation that was being planned, and thought that we were just going through the motions.

However, I knew that I was not always privy to the 'big picture' and discovered that certain people knew who was dealing in what, but in the best interests things were sometimes just allowed 'to let it run'. This was a term that the police liked to use whenever there was a big plan afoot. But at what point do you say enough is enough?

That was the problem with intelligence: no one really knew what was going on. All the handlers had their own informants and nothing happened unless the handlers authorised it, to keep their informants free from exposure. I think the handlers even kept information away from each other, and their office was always locked. There was always an undercurrent of someone being on the 'take', especially when an Op had been unsuccessful. When vast amounts of money are involved, temptation is always just below the surface.

However, that said, I never had any reason to suspect the men and women in the AIT and the handlers were anything other than police officers of the highest integrity.

During my time on AIT, we all went out socialising quite a lot, and one night we all went to The Comedy Store to watch a show. We all had quite a bit to drink during the show and I got merry but I wasn't drunk. As I left the venue with a colleague, we walked past the door to a nightclub. Now our intention was to get a taxi to take us home and the taxi rank was close by. We walked past the door to the nightclub and almost immediately I was assaulted by door staff outside the club entrance. To cut a long story short, I ended up being arrested for assault by my fellow police officers, one of whom was an Alpha sh*t, and taken to another police station some miles away.

I remember being placed in front of the custody sergeant who didn't quite know what to do.

He had been forewarned by the control room that a serving copper was being brought in for committing an assault. As an AIT officer I was seen by some as being part of an elite squad and so the custody sergeant wanted to make sure that procedures were strictly adhered to. He asked me if I wanted a solicitor and I said, "Yes." I wanted the 'worst solicitor', the one that we, the Old Bill, all hated: I wanted him. The custody sergeant knew what I meant and set the wheels in motion.

Unbeknown to me, a police sergeant had gone into the nightclub where the incident occurred, and seized the video evidence of me being assaulted. The doormen had all lied in their statements to the investigating officers and the video showed that quite clearly. But at the time I was oblivious to all this. I remember being locked up in a cell and I broke down in tears. My teenage daughter was at home on her own at the time and I was worried because I knew she would be worried about her dad. I sobered up very quickly and tried to recount the incident in my mind and was sure I hadn't committed any offence. I finally got to sleep and was woken up in the morning by the custody sergeant carrying a cup of tea. He told me that the solicitor, 'the worst one', he said with a smile, was on his way. After a short time, I eventually spoke with the solicitor who reassured me that he had seen the video of the incident and couldn't understand why I was still being held in police custody. He confirmed that I was OK to be interviewed and reminded me to keep my answers short and not to elaborate. And, most of all, not to lose my temper or get too cocky.

So we both went into the interview room. It was strange because I now knew what it felt like to be on the other side of the table, so to speak. Instead of being a police officer and carrying out the interview, I was now the suspect being on the receiving end.

So the interview starts with two Professional Standards officers (senior police officers who investigate other police officers), my solicitor and myself. After being interviewed by the Professional Standards for about an hour, it became apparent that there had been a serious cock-up on their part, i.e. the police. They couldn't find anything to substantiate a probable reason why I had been arrested and held in a police prison cell all night.

After the interview had finished, I was bailed for four weeks for further evidence to be obtained. My solicitor took me aside and had a quiet word in my ear. He said that they had nothing on me and that he doubted he would ever see me again, implying that it was all a farce. So after getting a lift home by Pro Standards I went back to work where I found myself suspended, pending the result of my case. Finally, after six weeks, I was told that no further action would be instigated against me. I was to be fully exonerated of any crime and that nothing detrimental would be written in my personal file. Big deal: I was so angry.

I was finally shown the video of the incident captured by the nightclub's surveillance cameras, and it quite clearly showed that I had done nothing wrong. Why the f@@k had I been arrested in the first place? Wrongful arrest, sue them, sue them, burn the mothers, and similar thoughts entered my mind. During those six weeks, the job offered me counselling. Now this is a double-edged ploy by the police. Under H&S, and the fact they don't want to be sued, they offer counselling, knowing full well that an officer would initially decline the offer. The reason is that any officer accepting counselling can kiss their career goodbye. So the powers that be know that most officers are more likely to say, "No thanks," and soldier on. At the time, mistakenly, it was looked upon as a weakness by the job. But I didn't give a damn about the job, so I rebelled and took six sessions of counselling paid for by Thames Valley Police.

I think it helped me tremendously. I was sceptical at first, but the counsellor was very good and for the first time since being arrested I was able to speak to someone who was totally independent.

He didn't judge me and didn't suggest I should sue for wrongful arrest (unlike many of my colleagues had): he just listened. He also explained to me that he had many police officers as patients. He never hinted at any names, rank or police force, just that there were many officers who had received counselling. More than the police would openly admit to. I can see the headlines in the local tabloids:

"COPS ON COUNSELLING"
"Studies show that 10% of all cops have had counselling sessions".

It doesn't send a good advert to the general public regarding the ability of the police. I was finally interviewed by the 'big cheeses', the detective chief inspector (my bosses' bosses' boss) and the head of personnel and was basically told to clear my desk, do not pass GO etc.

I was informed by them that the organisation (the police) was the most important thing and that my minor grievances were of no significance. It's not about the individual, but the good name of the force that's the most important thing, I was informed. I really felt like shit and replied that it's the individuals that make the organisation. I was brushed away with a stroke of a hand and was asked if this was really the career for me. Even though it's supposed to be confidential that you've received counselling, they had obviously got wind of it and decided to treat me like a leper. So I cleared my desk and ended up being downgraded to a department that consisted of the sick, lame, naughty and bad officers called the Service Delivery Office (SDU).

I had my last session with my counsellor shortly after the interview with the big cheeses and I told him about my imminent transfer. I told him how angry I was and he gave me a gem of advice. Basically do the best that you can and this will really annoy them. Because by putting me in the SDU they thought I would not be able to stand the indignity of working with such a bunch of misfit officers. How wrong the big cheeses were. I was now a misfit officer.

I initially thought I would not last dealing with the victims of low-level petty crime. Shoplifting, minor theft, minor assaults, theft of a flowerpot etc. Crime that was reported by the great unwashed and had to be dealt with. So who better to deal with these crimes than officers with a 'reputation'? All crimes that were reported and funnelled out as non-urgent or even 'OK, you've reported this incident but you ain't seeing an officer' were dealt with by the SDU. Some star jobs that rang my bell at the time were:

A report of a domestic assault, a husband of 75 phoning the police accusing his wife of bending his thumbs back. Apparently when she nagged him, he would cover his ears. She got so incensed with her husband's behaviour that she bent his thumbs. It was crimed as a domestic assault and we attended the address and dealt with it appropriately.

Another top job was a man reporting his cat's anus had human pubic hair attached. Result: police attendance.

This one was a 'top job'. A man reporting to the police to complain that he had to perform cunnilingus on his wife three times a day, otherwise she wouldn't feed him. They were both in their eighties. Result: domestic, police attendance.

These and many, many more jobs of a similar vein were the type of quality that the SDU were dumped with. After a short time I got to understand how it all worked and quite enjoyed it. I knew how stretched our precious resources were and if I could deal with something on the phone then I believed it would free up officers to go and chase proper criminals. However, as we were no longer a police force and now a police service – the difference being that the later dealt with crime, and the former dealt with everything under the sun, and dealing with crime was a side issue – the policy was that we should attend to everything.

The people who come up with the catchy latest police phrases always made us mere mortals raise our eyes and say, "What the fuck now?" and "What's the latest buzzword?" Has anyone noticed that there are absolutely no police officers on the streets anymore? They are all at the station writing reports and keeping their heads below the parapet.

Each day the SDU would get an allocation of three officers from shift to help with our enquiries.

These officers ranged from 'shit-hot' to downright laziest of the laziest. Because of the political climate, the police didn't attract people who wanted to police and make a positive contribution to society. It attracted mostly, but not always, university graduates who couldn't get a job, and policing seemed to be a substitute stopgap until something better came along. However, this analogy did not apply to all. So most of the officers on shift were in their twenties with little or no life skills. Very bright, but with very little good, old-fashioned copper skills like, 'Something isn't right, I'm gonna pursue this,' etc. Alas, that type of good, old-fashioned policing has now gone. Instead we have an organisation, the police force, that is in name only. However, in saying that, I did encounter some really good young officers, both men and women, who were destined for better things.

In its drive to cover all bases and tackle the 'domestic issue', the government put in place a new set of laws and legislation pertaining to the 'domestic umbrella'. Some typical scenarios that we dealt with were:

A) Two teenage sisters having an argument over the TV remote control. Domestic. Result: arrest them both.

B) A man sending his ex-wife a snotty text because she wouldn't let him see the kids. Domestic. Result: arrest him.

C) Two adult men having an argument over their business: one was stealing money from the business; the other one called him a useless c***. Domestic. Result: arrest him.

The list goes on and on and is totally and utterly pointless, unless of course you happen to be into the stats (statistics). Then, arresting all these offenders who have committed a domestic puts a totally misleading, warped angle on things.

It makes the police look as though it's tackling a rather nasty crime when in fact police officers are so tied up with dealing with the drivel dross that they haven't got the time to deal with the proper serious domestic offences. Like when someone really does need our help because of physical or mental abuse that they are suffering from.

In the last few years I have read a few Dan Brown books and similar, relating to all manner of conspiracy theories. It's easy to believe some of these theories because the experiences that I have witnessed made me think, 'Who the fuck is actually running this clusterfuck? Are they for real?'

In my last six months in the job, the SDU were abandoned. This was really surprising because only a few years previously the SDUs were the 'foundation of policing' and the 'underpin of policing' – yes, these buzzwords were used relentlessly in the new millennium by senior police officers.

So after the demise of the SDU I got promoted to being the Hate Crime Coordinator for the North Bucks Area. 'Hate crime' were now the new buzzwords and anything relating to a crime with a hate element was jumped on with all guns blazing. It was the biggest farce yet. I could write a short book on the utter total waste of time and money in the history of modern policing. The real crime was that occasionally, and I stress occasionally, we actually had a crime with a serious hate element in it. Someone actually being the victim of an assault because of their colour or race, religion etc: a proper hate crime. But for the most part it was all very petty stuff done up to look like we had a hate crime epidemic. Don't forget it was all about the 'stats'.

So a minor incident like name-calling between schoolkids and someone shouts, "Why don't you go back where you belong?" etc, we allocated officers like they were going out of fashion.

Every morning I had to attend the 9 o'clock meeting, aka morning prayers, and explain to the hierarchy what hate crimes had been reported to the police in the last 24 hours, and who had been arrested. It didn't matter how many hate crimes were reported as long as we could say we solved the crime, then that's all that mattered.

There was a procedure called 'getting rid of a crime' and I became a master of the dark arts in getting rid of a crime in a short time. All hate crimes were monitored by staff at headquarters (HQ) and I had many a run-in with the number-crunchers at HQ, arguing that an incident had been attended and it could be written off as either solved or no further action.

It really was a game. No one really cared about the actual crime, it was just about 'getting a result'.

So the police could say that hate crime was down by 50%, or we had increased arrests by 28% – whatever, it was all about the stats. I dealt with some ridiculous incidents, but my best had to be the Chris Evans incident. A caller wanted to report a hate crime because Chris Evans had allegedly said, "Dago" on his radio show. The caller complained to Radio 2, but apparently they told him to fuck off and get a life, in so many words. So he complained to us, the police, and we went ahead and crimed the ruddy report as a hate crime due to its racist connotations. You've got to laugh. So an officer had to go and see the caller and take a statement, and what? Go to London and arrest Mr Evans? No, it was filed and I had to explain to the senior management at morning prayers what I was doing about it and how the investigation was progressing. Obviously it took all my skills in the dark arts to get rid of that pile of crap.

I really got my head around the government's piece of legislation regarding 'hate crime': after all, I was supposed to be the guru on this subject. Basically if an individual thinks it's a hate crime, i.e. a racist incident, a homophobic incident, an anti-religious incident, anti-colour incident, anti-country of origin incident, or anti-disability incident, then it's classified as a hate crime – in which case an officer would attend and take a statement from the caller and carry out numerous enquiries, sometimes taking weeks, after which the alleged offender might be arrested. So you can insult anybody, but do not use any connotations involving the above, then there's no hate crime.

But here's the kicker: you can say anything you like in your own home, even to a police officer (that's of course if they haven't come to arrest you) and it has to be inside your house and not on your doorstep, then there's no hate crime. The only proviso is that if anyone outside your house hears what you have to say then it becomes a hate crime. So if you do decide to have a rant, then say it quietly.

There were serious assaults reported to the police that had to wait because a hate crime took priority over a non-hate crime, immaterial of the severity of the crime. So someone reports that a neighbour has shouted, "Go back from where you came from!" or something similar, then this would be recorded as a hate crime. At the same time somebody else reports that they've been punched in the face for no apparent reason. The hate crime would get priority and the victim of the assault would have to wait sometimes for days to see an officer, after which any forensic evidence would have disappeared and the original complainant of the assault would have probably given up waiting to see a police officer.

I remember the John Terry/Anton Ferdinand incident where Terry was supposed to have said, "You fucking black cunt." The CPS went for a Section 4 Racially Aggravated Public Order (RAPO). I knew straight away that he would be found not guilty: the CPS solicitor and their bosses who allowed it were all fools. It should have been a Sect 5 RAPO: big difference. His (Terry's) solicitor was laughing all the way to the Leeds – or was that the Chelsea?

It was during this period that I met a truly wonderful person who came to be my third and final wife. How privileged and lucky I was to have met such a wonderful lady and one who would put up with me.

With 'Lewis' a guard dog on my basic training course, Melton Mowbray 1978

With Lotus, at an army base in Londonderry 1978/79

7 Platoon, (the well-ards) Londonderry 1983/84

Smart boy, Mlton Keynes 1986.

Proud boy at the time. 1992, after passing out at the police training school

In the stocks at a local summer fete trying to raise money for the local community. 1995/96

Completion of my RMP basic training, 1995

Eton college control room protecting the young royals, 1999/2000

With Chalky, Gibbo and Tonka just completing some serious tree felling,
Spain 2016

A special day with Sue. Stony Stratford. 2014

CHAPTER 10

I finally left the Old Bill in January 2011 and I'm not sure if I had any great regrets. Serving in the police was somewhat disappointing. Admittedly in the early days, the 1990s, I felt the police force made a positive difference to people's lives. Now I'm not too sure. I like to think I made a mainly positive impact on people's lives and was thought highly of by most of my peers in the police. I would say that the vast majority of coppers whom I had the privilege to serve with were outstanding individuals. Unfortunately, that cannot be said for all, as I did serve with a mixture of plonkers, bullshitters and some very strange individuals who you had to wonder how they ever managed to get into the police in the first place. But thankfully they were in the minority.

So I handed in my ID card and walked out of the gates of the police station for the last time and felt absolutely nothing. Now, this worried me a little because I thought maybe I'm going to really miss this and that I was in a delayed shock. So I waited and waited – and nothing. 18 years and ten months give or take, and I was a free man again. Or so I thought.

I once read that society gets the police that it deserves. So maybe it's all our fault that we have the service that we have.

After I left the police I did the usual things that one does. I learnt to sail, and sailed around the Isle of Wight. I learnt to canoe and did white water rafting in South America. I also walked the Inca Trail to Machu Picchu in Peru with my wife. We did the full 26 miles and it took us four days to complete the epic journey. Meeting the Inca people, who were our guides and the porters who also carried the majority of our kit, was an eye-opener. They were so humble, and it made me realise how lucky I was. They ranged in age from their late-teens to late-forties, all were thin and small, but very strong and durable. We overnourished, overweight Westerners, with all our fancy footwear and clothing, struggled with just a backpack to carry. These little chaps would literally run past us, carrying the bulk of everyone's kit, all the campaign gear, the portable kitchen, the Portaloos, and just wearing flip-flops or badly worn trainers, shorts and an old tee shirt.

There were approximately 20 Westerners in our party and we all made it, the full 26 miles. It really was an endurance test both mental and physical, but what a great feeling we all had when we saw Machu Picchu for the first time on the morning of the fourth day.

Our two guides were Inca people and both spoke English. They explained that the porters (also Incas) relied heavily on the tips that they received from us Westerners, to feed their families. All of us in the party tipped generously and we had a peep when our guide handed them the money on the evening of day 3. They were like small children receiving a present from Santa, it really was a humbling moment. (20 dollars is a week's pay to these people.) Apparently, when they reach a certain age, they have to stop being porters because of the strenuous nature of the work. When this happens, they can go into deep depression because there is very little left for them to do. I will always recall the shouts of "Porters coming!" When you heard this, everyone in the party would stand to one side of the narrow path, usually the side of the mountain, and let the porters run past us. When we eventually arrived at our base camp, the porters would have set up our tents, rolled out our sleeping bags, and a meal would be cooking for us. They even made a couple of birthday cakes for two of the walkers in our party, as both had a birthday whilst walking the Inca Trail.

Whenever I feel a little sorry for myself, I have a little think of those

Porters and the life they have had. The thing is, they always looked happy, I bet they weren't.

I tried to get tickets for the 2012 London Olympic but every time I tried to log on, I couldn't get any of the tickets for the events that I wanted to see. So instead, I ended up applying with G4S to work at the Olympics. I filed in the application form and went along to their opening day. This was held at Upton Park, the home of West Ham United Football Club. G4S had the contract to supply the security at many of the sporting events. One word springs to mind: shambles. At least I got to see some of the Olympic competitions and had a great laugh, even though G4S were truly rubbish – but they paid well.

My dear old mum departed from this world in October 2012. The ceremony was held at her local church and afterwards we went to the local crematorium. I think I miss her more now that she's gone than I ever did when she was alive. I know there's a moral there somewhere.

After a few odd jobs I finally got a job with a company called Tascor. They worked in conjunction with the Immigration Service and had the contract from the government to remove failed asylum seekers from the UK and return them to their country of birth. We also removed criminals from the UK who were foreign nationals, and finally we took back overstayers. They were people whose visas had expired and who had refused to go back to their country of origin voluntarily. If G4S were a shambles, then Tascor managed to surpass that description. The management were totally incompetent, except for one or two exceptions who somehow managed to paper over the cracks. We were called 'overseas escorts' and normally there would be three escorts taking a detainee back. One escort would be the team leader, responsible for running the operation, then a further two escorts who were responsible for the detainee. On occasions there would be four of us taking a detainee back, especially if he was particularly violent or he was a self-harmer. These were called kickers, shiters, biters and fighters. You get the gist.

On occasions we would have a medic to administer first aid and to confirm that the detainee was fit to fly. We would use commercial flights to take our detainees back and sometimes this caused controversy, because our person more often than not would decide to 'kick off'. Shouting, swearing, screaming, threatening, kicking the back of the seat, being as disruptive as possible, so the captain would say to us, "No way, get off the plane." When this happened, which was quite frequently, we would have to take the detainee back to a secure unit and then start all over again with the removal. On a rare occasion, the flight captain would be informed beforehand that the detainee would be difficult. It was music to our ears when we heard them say, "No problem, we'll take them no matter what." I will mention a couple of memorable jobs that I was involved with during my time with the company.

Taking a 73-year-old Philippine lady back to Manila after she had been in the UK for 55 years. She had children and grandchildren here in the UK and had worked as a cleaner and nanny all her life in this country. But she was an overstayer, having come here 55 years ago on a one-year visa, and had stayed here illegally ever since. Now you tell me, did the Home Office get that one right?

Taking a particularly nasty individual back to Jamaica. He was a career criminal who came to the UK illegally, committed numerous violent crimes, but refused to go home because his human rights would be violated. It took five of us to carry him onto the plane because he put such up a fight, and he especially hated me, saying I was a traitor to the black man, and that I was a coconut. I sat next to him for most of the flight and he did nothing but give me the 'evils' throughout. I wonder how he's doing.

On another flight to Jamaica, we were asked by the cabin crew if we could help them with a violent passenger. Our detainee was a 'big unit', but calm and peaceful. So we left one escort and the medic with our man, and the team leader and myself went with the cabin crew to confront whatever hell-like passenger who had caused so much panic.

We were told that this passenger was in first-class and he had been drinking for two hours and had become violent and threatening and had taken over the bar in first-class. The captain was so concerned that he intended to divert to New York and hand the aggressor over to the

US authorities. So we followed the cabin crew through the aircraft and up to first-class and saw this drunken, aggressive man behind the bar with the cabin crew almost cowering. (They weren't paid enough to be assaulted by drunken violent men.)

My colleague and I then told matey boy to follow us back to his seat. At first he complied and we walked him back to where his seat was in first-class. The captain then put the 'fasten seat belts' sign on, so we told matey boy to put his seat belt on and stay in his seat. He did this and we left him there and walked back to the bar area and told staff that if they needed our help again, not to hesitate and come and get us. All of a sudden matey boy appears next to us and punches me to the side of the jaw. After a second of shock, I grabbed hold of him and handcuffed him, after which he was frogmarched back to his seat and an extended constraint belt was found and we wrapped this around him and fastened him to his seat.

There were 13 other passengers in first-class and they all cheered except for one. The one abstainer was matey boy's wife, who was equally drunk but not abusive. My colleague and I took turns in staying with matey boy: after all, we did have a detainee to look after. Luckily for us, he was as good as gold. For the next four hours matey boy started to sober up and when we were about 30 minutes from our destination he was almost sober. At first I couldn't identify his nationality because of his cursing and swearing. As he sobered up he was appalled by his behaviour. He told me that he was a recovering alcoholic and been on the wagon for six months. The free booze on offer was too much of a temptation and he succumbed to his demons by throwing back the free alcohol like it was going out of fashion. He was very apologetic and embarrassed by his actions.

However, when we landed a giant Jamaican policewoman and her equally large male colleague were waiting for matey boy. We were later told that he was arrested and banned from all further Virgin Atlantic flights.

The good karma to come out of this episode was that Virgin Atlantic gave me another 12 months' Gold membership. So cheap flights on

Virgin Atlantic and more access to the lounges.

I could write a book on the experiences I had with the company as an overseas escort. I did it for three and a half years, but there were some escorts that had been doing the job in one capacity or another for more than 15 years.

In essence there were a lot of good people who were escorts and team leaders. There was also a considerable amount of incompetence by some escorts, the management and the system in general. It really was a shambles at times. The company's mantra is communication; well, I saw and heard very little of this in my time with them. For example:

We would go to get our tickets for a flight and would often be told by the airline that we had arrived on the wrong day. Our flights were booked for the following day.

Detainees with no paperwork, so we couldn't fly them home.

Escorts with the wrong travel docs or an incorrect entry visa. Very embarrassing.

Turning up at an immigration centre only to be told by staff that the detainee wasn't there and that they had no idea where our detainee was.

Arriving at the immigration centre without a medic when the paperwork says, 'medic required'. No medic: job gets cancelled.

Getting on wrong planes, very embarrassing.

The list is endless. However, in spite of all these hurdles (mainly self-inflicted), we did manage to get a good proportion of detainees back to their original county. I think a lot of good people were removed out of the country wrongly, but as I'm not privy to the bigger picture, maybe there are circumstances that I'm not aware of.

I got married in August 2014 to a wonderful lady called Sue. We had a fantastic wedding ceremony, and went on a cruise around the Med for our honeymoon. I could write a separate book about our 'Big Day' – maybe another time.

I finely left Tascor in October 2017 for my latest venture which is a part-time supporting artiste, or 'extras', as we're better known, working on films and TV. To date I've been in three films and a small number of TV dramas, and I love it.

I sometimes have to remind myself how lucky I was to have been trained by the best. The British Army, Class 1 of 72, Bassingbourn Barracks. I looked up the word 'training' in the dictionary. Basics, education, guidance, instruction, discipline, upbringing and drill were just a few of the words to describe this. I would say that the Army's training was all these and more.

How lucky I was to have enlisted as a junior soldier all those years ago.

The End

If after reading this book, only one person gets inspired and turns their life around for the better, then It'll have been worth it.